D1386956

IMPLICIT RELIGION:
an introduction

Edward Bailey

**Centre for the Study of Implicit Religion
and Contemporary Spirituality
Middlesex University, White Hart Lane,
London   N17 8HR**

First published in 1998 by
Middlesex University Press

Middlesex University Press is an imprint of
Middlesex University Services Limited,
Bounds Green Road, London N11 2NQ

A CIP catalogue record for this book is available from
The British Library

ISBN 1 898253 24 2

Manufacture coordinated in UK from the
publisher's CRC by Book-in-Hand Ltd
London N6 5AH

CONTENTS

Acknowledgements   iv

THE IDEA

Chapter 1   How real is implicit religion?   4
              Transcendent experiences - Absolute values -
              Religious experiences - As empirical data - A
              fact of human life

Chapter 2   Why call it 'implicit religion'?   14
              'Religion' used neutrally - 'Implicit religion' a
              hypothesis - The popular use of 'religious' -
              The significance of 'implicit'

Chapter 3   What does 'implicit religion' mean?   21
              The needle in the haystack -
              Three definitions

Chapter 4   What is closest to implicit religion?   26
              'Civil religion' - 'Popular religion' - 'Folk religion'
              - 'Invisible religion'

i

ITS APPLICATION

Chapter 5   Implicit religion: in individuals   44
              The interviews - Commitments
                           - The analysis

Chapter 6   Implicit religion: in a public house   51
              The observation - Integrating foci
                           - The public house

Chapter 7   Implicit religion: in a suburb   59
              The participation - Intensive concerns with
              extensive effects

ITS IMPORTANCE

Chapter 8   Explicit religion and implicit religion   70
              'Implicit' or 'Explicit' religion the analogy? -
              Religion explicitly secondary

Chapter 9   Spiritual education and implicit religion 74
              'Spiritual' historically - 'spiritual' today

Chapter 10   The future and implicit religion   78

APPENDICES

Invitation 1   To relate religion, consciousness and   84
                experience

Invitation 2   To analyse the interview data   85

Invitation 3   To further reading and study   110

Acknowledgements

I would like to express my gratitude to Kok Pharos Publishing House for permission to reprint the Interviews from my *Implicit Religion in Contemporary Society* (1997), and to *Daedalus: Journal of the American Academy of Arts and Sciences* for permission to quote from Robert Bellah's *Civil Religion in America*, and to Collier-MacMillan, to quote from Thomas Luckmann's *Invisible Religion*.

The publication of *Implicit Religion in Contemporary Society*, early in 1997, provided a public opportunity to express my gratitude to many who had helped, over the preceding thirty years, with the odyssey for the recognition of the reality of 'implicit religion'. Some had been specifically involved, up-front or behind the scenes, with the activities of the Network for the Study of Implicit Religion, which was formalised in 1985. It also gave me the chance to say that there were many more than I could name.

I would like to reiterate all those acknowledgements in this, the first short volume of Introduction to implicit religion. To them, however, I would like to add all those who have helped to find a landing-place for its study. In particular, one thinks of Ninian Smart, who suggested that Middlesex University might provide a suitable port, and of Tim Putnam and Christopher Lamb, who, as Professor of Research and Head of the Centre for Inter-Faith Dialogue respectively, piloted the vessel to its moorings. With them, on the enlarged board of trustees for the Centre for the Study of Implicit Religion and Contemporary Spirituality, I would like to thank Ken Goulding, the University's Deputy Vice-Chancellor, and, on the Management Committee of the Centre, Gabrielle Parker, the Head of the Faculty of Humanities and Cultural Studies, and Sheena Bradley-Barnes, David Dewey and Martin Eggleton, on the curricular working party. Then, behind the scenes, as ever, are so many others I would like to thank, such as Penelope Weald, Marie Hannam, and Ted Polson, and, connected with Middlesex University Press, John Annette, Colin Francome, Marion Locke, and others, all of whose willing helpfulness I would like to take this opportunity to acknowledge.

However, coupled with Middlesex University, I would also like to express my thanks to the Archbishop of Canterbury, Dr George Carey, who during the year kindly invited me to give my inaugural lecture, as the University's visiting professor in implicit religion, at Lambeth Palace.

So, with gratitude for the welcome that has been given, and in recognition of the efficient flexibility of a new yet old institution, I would like to dedicate this little book, with a New Year toast, to ... 'the Archbishop, and Middlesex University'.

Edward Bailey, 1 January 1998
Winterbourne Rectory, Bristol

THE IDEA

I HOW REAL IS IMPLICIT RELIGION?

Some things we learn the name of, and then, afterwards, discover for ourselves in greater depth what the word really means. For instance knowing there is a place called Tottenham, we can go and see it for ourselves. Love and marriage, pain and grief, might be more serious examples.

Other things we can sense the existence of, even before we can name them. Poetry, for instance, often puts into words what we already knew to be true, but had no way of saying. The first way of knowing could be described as knowledge about, the second, as knowledge of.

Knowledge in the fullest sense will include both ways of knowing. However, in order to distinguish the two sides of what is, ideally, a single coin, we could call 'knowledge about', comprehension, and 'knowledge of', apprehension. 'Comprehension' is what we can know from the outside, by observing the behaviour and relationships within the relevant context. 'Apprehension' is what we can know from the inside, by empathetically penetrating the beings themselves.

This book's other chapters will all focus on comprehending implicit religion. The following three chapters, for instance, will describe its meaning, by asking why this particular name has been given to it, and how it can be defined, and what other terms have been used, to point in approximately the same direction. The trio after that will report upon three ways in which the concept has been given practical application: by interviewing individuals, by observing the life of a public house, and by taking part in the life of a residential community. The final three chapters will position implicit religion within its context, by sketching its relationship with explicit religion, with spiritual education, and with some current pointers towards future developments.

This chapter, however, is more concerned with apprehending implicit religion. Because some people think of it primarily in terms of a sort of secular mysticism, it begins by trying to describe what is meant by a 'transcendent experience', in the sense of what it is like actually to experience one. It then talks about 'absolute values', in the sense of what it is like, to value anything, in

4

that way. Next, it looks at what we call specifically 'religious experiences', as recorded by the Jewish prophet Isaiah, as analysed by the German theologian Otto, and as seen by the French sociologist Durkheim.

In conclusion, the chapter suggests that such 'unusual' moments are now known to be quite common; it enquires how they are related to the rest of experience; but it emphasises that 'implicit religion' tends to be more concerned with the 'sticking-points' that are to be found in ordinary life, than with such 'extraordinary' experiences. For the object of this chapter is to bring to the surface those largely hidden 'rocks' upon which (so far as we can) we try to build our lives. Because we have difficulty in describing these inner bedrocks of people's own intentionality, their 'implicit religion', we otherwise run the risk of overlooking the very source of their identity.

APPREHENSION

Transcendent experiences

During the twentieth century we have learned again to pay attention to what we call the unconscious and the subconscious. We are aware, for instance, that when we recount last night's dream, we are not simply describing an incomprehensible, because illogical, fantasy: we are also revealing something of our own, inner life, albeit a part over which we have little control.

As the century draws to a close, we are beginning to take increasing interest in our experiences at what might be described as the other end of the spectrum. These are moments, or longer periods, when we have a heightened awareness of our surroundings, and/or of ourselves. They may come to us when we suddenly 'see' (for ourselves, the wonder of) a flower, or 'real-ise' (within ourselves, more fully) the meaning of love, or experience an unusual creativity.

Such experiences were often seen as religious. Certainly, like dreams, at the other end of the spectrum, they are difficult to understand, in the terms of ordinary, middle-of-the-road consciousness. So they tended, either to be equated with experiences of the divine (or of some approximation to divinity), or else to be ignored (or 'explained', i.e. explained *away*). What 'Enlightenment' ways of thinking shed no light on (as with the so called 'Dark Ages'), they (inevitably) tended to dismiss, as both unworthy and 'unreal'.

Nowadays we tend to call such experiences 'transcendent'. This nicely accommodates the conviction which their subjects often report, of having been brought into touch with a reality that was more, not less, real than the run-of-the-mill reality. At the same time it avoids committing itself to anything more than saying that the experience itself, though unusual, was real for its subject, and that it was not necessarily pathological. Thus it is recognised as a legitimate subject for study.

Because 'transcendent experiences' are (by definition) *un*-usual, they are hard to describe or to account for, in terms of ordinary life, consciousness and thought. Experiences of transcendence, in other words, are *sui generis* (in a class of their own). But certain common characteristics are apparent. Above all, for instance, it is always difficult to describe both the experience of the experience (what seemed to happen), and its content. It is also difficult to explain why such experiences happen, when they are likely to happen, or to whom they happen. They seem to be both indescribable or ineffable, and inexplicable or irreducible.

However, the very sense of their importance encourages some of those who have had such experiences, to try and describe both the experience and the content. From these descriptions we can say that they are usually short-lived - a matter of minutes, or even seconds. Indeed, fifteen of the famous *Sixteen Revelations of Divine Love* that Julian of Norwich received on the 8 May 1375, apparently happened within five hours, while the sixteenth itself came next day.

It also seems as though the subject's own heightened sense of consciousness, is part and parcel of a similarly heightened sense of the reality of its object. In the old testament, when Moses' attention was drawn to the 'burning' bush in the desert (Exodus 3:1-6), for instance, his own awareness and awe may have exactly paralleled his intense realisation that the bush combined facticity with fragility.

When it comes to 'explaining' such experiences, their subjects tend to see them as an act of grace (like existence as a whole). They seem just to arrive, 'out of the blue'. Nevertheless, we can suggest certain generalisations. For instance, they may be sparked off by something in nature, or in human life, such as beauty, or danger. In either case, this could 'account for' the sense of their sheer, unwarranted graciousness.

This, in turn, suggests that, just as the subject's description reflects the character of the experience, so the content of the experience will reflect the concepts the subjects themselves already possess. This does not mean that the experience is necessarily merely a creation of their expectation and imagination. It only means that they cannot report, and may not even be able to experience, what they cannot even imagine. The experience itself remains unexpected.

A second generalisation reflects the sense of novelty, uniqueness, value and 'revelation' that accompanies such experiences: they tend to occur in childhood, adolescence, or early adulthood, when we are particularly likely to be discovering new things in, or new qualities to, or new dimensions of, life. In the 1970s and '80s, for instance, when it first became usual for fathers to be present at the birth of their children, they often wanted to share their sense of awe at the experience. Some doctors say they feel the same way, every time.

A third generalisation that we can make, however, regarding the occurrence of such an experience, is its unpredictability. It may be possible to produce emotional or psychological experiences, by lack of food or sleep for instance, but 'transcendent' experiences have to be related to the environment, as well as the subject's own mind. One of the Roman Catholic Church's criteria for true sanctity, for instance, has been permanent growth in moral attitude. Transcendent experiences, if they are actually *of* transcendence, are not only empirical (and therefore available for study), but are also expected to have pragmatic (ie practical and observable) results. Their reality is not simply mental and self-contained.

Absolute values

'Transcendent' experiences can spark off a poem - or occur in the process of writing it. Indeed, if 'art' refers to *how* we do things (eg set out a page of type, or serve food), then 'great art' could refer to

7

the ways in which such experiences are evoked or provoked in us. So we can describe either their content, or its communication, as 'beautiful'.

No doubt it was experiences of this sort, on his own part or on the part of others, that led Plato, in the fifth century BCE, to value beauty so highly. Indeed, in view of the suddenness, and the heights, of his contemporaries' achievements, in such 'dedicated' (non-utilitarian) art-forms as drama, sculpture and architecture, it is hardly surprising that he should have described the value of beauty as 'absolute'. Conversely, we confess to kindred feelings, in the face of wanton acts of destruction, when we have to call upon the title of a barbarian tribe (the Vandals), in order to refer to behaviour that (people say) leaves them 'speechless'.

Presumably Plato reflected his own dedication to philosophy (literally, the 'love of wisdom'), when he put Truth alongside Beauty, as an absolute value. If today we tend to value truth less highly than he did, that may be because we tend both to define it more narrowly, and to see it as a means to an end, such as the prevention of unnecessary suffering. We may still, however, feel that truth has an absolute quality, which gives it some kind of claim upon us. We sense that we should follow where it leads, even when this seems inconvenient to us, rather than just using it for our own ends.

Plato's third absolute, Goodness, has tended to go up in general esteem. Seen as Love, and always high in popular esteem, it has certainly become the easy way of justifying attention to Beauty and Truth - in terms of human welfare and happiness. However, Plato's own sense that Goodness is intrinsically good, regardless of its consequences, may account for part of our reaction to the abuse of children, for instance, or to violence against ambulance or aid workers.

What we value, depends upon our own experience. (The influence of that evaluation upon our behaviour, however, may also depend upon our ability to justify our intuitions, to ourselves and others.) *That* we all value some things, independently of any price we may have paid, is now recognised, for instance by people who want to know what price we will pay for 'goods' of any kind. (Those who said, 'Every man has his [financial] price', may have been simply generalising from their own awareness.) So long as people have to make choices between what they *want* to happen (as against guesses, as to what will happen, willy-nilly), they cannot avoid prioritising their preferences, and so exhibiting a value system. Within that hierarchy, while some of our 'objects' may seem relatively arbitrary or optional, others may seem to be 'given' or 'self-evident'. To the holder, if to no one else, they are part of the way existence *is*, as well as the way it should be.

Religious experiences

Plato's trio of Absolutes stand for one entire strand within human life. They could be described as the epitome of philosophy. Another strand is summed up in the Jewish prophet Isaiah's triplet, 'Holy, holy, holy', which we might paraphrase as, 'God, you are God indeed, and you alone are God'. It could be described as the epitome of religion.

Sometimes it seems as though individuals and cultures opt for either the Greek trio or else the Hebrew one. Philosophy seems to concentrate on speaking *about* what is ultimately real, religion on speaking *to* it. However, the apparent difference may partly reflect our own limitations. Each may be necessary to complete the other.

Plato's three Absolutes may look like three divinities. In which case (if this is a uni-verse) we may look for some way of relating them to each other - and for some development of their relationship with us. Isaiah's trisagion ('thrice-holy') may look splendidly single-minded. In which case (if creation is also gloriously diverse), we may look for some validation of its parts.

Perhaps this is why the famous 13th Chapter of St Paul's First Letter to the Corinthians in the 'New Testament' appeals both so widely and so directly, almost 'by-passing' the rational mind. Speaking (in Buddha-like terms), of what is 'permanent' rather than 'absolute', he names a different trio: faith, hope and charity. But, in prioritising the last, he avoids any danger of either polytheism or iconoclasm, by pointing towards a unified hierarchy of values. Each of them has an absolute quality, but none of them is absolute in itself. *Relatively* divine, they each possess a dimension of divinity, and point beyond themselves.

9

Such formulae echo Einstein's $e=mc^2$: their relevance is inversely ubiquitous to their brevity. But their brevity is not the only reason for their popularity. They appeal because they clearly speak for people, as well as to them. For apprehensions, whether of a transcendent dimension, or of an absolute value, or of communicated divinity, are far more common than we used to realise. Indeed, if it were not for the high valuation placed upon them, and their importance in understanding people, we might be tempted to dismiss them, not because they were unreal, but because they are commonplace.

As empirical data

At the very beginning of the century, in 1901-2, William James' Gifford Lectures, *The Varieties of Religious Experience*, set the scene for the empirical study of such discrete data. More pertinent to the religious dimension within ordinary life, however, is Rudolph Otto's *Das Heilige* [The Holy], published in (of all years) 1917. Translated as early as 1923, its English title, *The Idea [sic] of the Holy*, almost exactly contradicted its thesis: that humans can apprehend a *mysterium tremendum et fascinans* (an overwhelming yet fascinating mystery) which is *sui generis* and *prior to* (rather than consequent upon) all other ideas, even moral ones.

In order to name this mystery (as he had to), he coined a phrase, 'the numinous', from the Latin word *numen*. Referring to a deity's nod-of-the-head, it points to the sense of a divine will and power that is present in such '*numinous* experiences'. The new word's rapid incorporation into the language, indicates the need for a term to describe such experiences, on the part of many who know nothing of Latin or of Rudolph Otto.

As it happens, a very similar conclusion had been published a mere two years before Otto's *Das Heilige*. In 1912, from the opposite side in the 'Great War', *Les Formes Elementaires de la Vie Religieuse* was published in French, and in 1915 in English, as 'The Elementary Forms of the Religious Life'. In it, Emile Durkheim suggested that religion, in the form of group rituals, engenders an ecstasy that provides a supreme contrast with ordinary consciousness, and so is prior to all conceptual distinctions. (This

10

basic bifurcation of consciousness, and its development, is set out diagrammatically, in the first of the appended 'Invitations'.)

The similarity of their conclusions (and near-simultaneity of their publications), was all the more remarkable in view of the contrast between both their starting-points and their core-interests. For Otto was a devout Lutheran professor of theology, interested in religious (including Hindu) mysticism, on the part of individuals. Durkheim, on the other hand, was an atheist Jewish professor of sociology, interested in social (including aboriginal) bonding.

If Otto's *datum* is an individual, seated in the nave of a medieval cathedral, while the organist plays Bach, Durkheim's *datum* is the primitive tribe, dancing round its totem. Independently, yet complementarily, each recognises the religious and social phenomena of the exterior of human life, and through it arrives at that interior life with which phenomenology is concerned, in order to observe the moment of 'nuclear fission' in human consciousness. In doing so, they anticipated the current concern with the presence of the 'spiritual' in every department of life.

A fact of human life
The statistical frequency of 'religious experience' still comes as a shock to some. For many of us were brought up in contexts in which, at least in public (in the mass media, or school textbooks), such experiences were either simply ignored, or else were dismissed, either as really something else, or else as dangerous. This 'censorship', whether conscious or unconscious, was indicative of the challenge to accustomed ways that they posed. When such experiences (unusual in each person's life-time, but very common among people as a whole) were reported, the ones chosen tended towards the dubious or the bizarre: suggesting that if they did occur, they were of doubtful veracity, or pathological in cause or effect. Not even the great religious leaders escaped that suspicion.

The work (summarised in David Hay's *Exploring Inner Space*) of the Religious Experience Research Unit at Oxford (now re-named, after its founder, the Alister Hardy Research Centre), since 1968, has been replicated in the USA. It shows that one-third of the population, if asked by a pollster in the street, will admit to having had a religious experience. It also shows that, if there is any error of interpretation, then the figure should be two thirds, not one third. However, 'admit' is said, advisedly. It indicates the frequency of the additional 'confession' that the experience had never been mentioned to anyone before, as the experience was believed by respondents to be uncommon, and might therefore lead to the person being thought 'odd'. Yet other evidence showed, on the contrary, that such experiences tended to accompany above-average psychological well-being (without suggesting the direction of any cause-and-effect relationship).

The recent willingness to investigate such experiences may be put on a par with the beginning of sustained study of near-death experiences and parapsychological phenomena in the same period. Such open-mindedness can be seen as part of that general cultural shift, which is often described in terms of a change from modernism to post-modernism. As an intellectual movement, combining objectivity with subjectivity, both in its observation and analysis, its 'open-mindedness' is welcome. It no more needs to be equated with 'woolly-mindedness', than 'catholicity' needs to be equated with 'fatalism'.

Implicit religion, then, is as real as these moments of heightened consciousness, whether they are understood in terms of transcendence, values or religion. But it is not restricted to such 'sur-conscious' experiences. It may be less obvious in times of ordinary consciousness; but it could be argued that it is more important then. It is revealed, for instance, when some one's (or some group's) basic beliefs about the way the world is or should be (which may hitherto have been unconscious, even to themselves) are affirmed ('Here I stand') - or are changed; when what we 'must' (or 'must not') do, has priority over what we merely 'can' (or 'cannot') do; and when we discover who is most profoundly 'one of us' (or 'not one of us'), and 'whose side we are on', 'when the chips are down'.

People can be largely understood in terms of causes and effects, both physical and psychological. But they are not just a bundle of pre-programmed reactions: they can respond to, and influence how they inter-act with, their inheritance and environment. Indeed, it is this capacity that simultaneously makes us more than merely natural ('super-natural'), and also makes everyone different

12

from everyone else - in their character, as well as their finger-prints. We recognise this when we try and 'put ourselves in their shoes', in order to understand them better.

It is this area, of unique intentionality, with which implicit religion is concerned. If we cannot understand some one's (or some group's) behaviour, we may ask what *they thought* they were doing: what was their expectation? In the same way, when someone dies, we may ask, not only what they did, but what they stood for. We do not expect them to have achieved their goal, but it helps us to understand them if we know what was in their mind. The study of implicit religion is based on the premise that it is better not to wait until they die, before asking such questions.

- Looking at case histories why
* do some respond in one way, +
Others another?

- What they did reflected what
they stood for - (if they were
able to make that choice?)

2   WHY CALL IT 'IMPLICIT RELIGION'?

There are, it must be admitted, some disadvantages in calling such 'sur-conscious' experiences or 'subconscious' assumptions, on the part of individuals or groups, *implicitly religious*.

'Religion' used neutrally

In the first place, it may give offence. The person who says, I am not religious, may resent being described as being religious, even 'implicitly'. Indeed, he may resent this all the more, because he may feel both that he is being told he doesn't really know himself, and also that no one can possibly avoid being religious. He may feel that he is being covertly trapped and pigeon-holed, despite his appraisal of himself as religiously inactive, or as 'unbelieving', or even (as Max Weber described himself), as being religiously 'tone-deaf'; or despite his deliberate and negative verdict upon religion, as obsolete, superfluous, or downright dangerous.

This fear can inspire a passion and clarity of thought that, in its turn, can arouse the sympathy of those who identify themselves as religious. (Durkheim would have recognised both stages in the process.)   Indeed, this is the reason for considering this disadvantage first. Some comments can be offered, however, in response to this complaint.

Most obvious is the need to reach an understanding of how 'religion' is being used. To be 'implicitly religious', in no way implies being 'implicitly Christian' (let alone, for example, being 'like people who say they don't believe in blood transfusion, based on what it says in the Bible').

Some of us may still sometimes 'catch ourselves out' equating 'England' with Britain or with the United Kingdom (or equating the Church of England with the Anglican Communion), and so on. Yet two centuries ago, Henry Fielding pointed out these distinctions, when he pictured Parson Thwackum as declaring, 'When I say religion, I mean the Christian religion, and when I say the Christian religion, I meant the Protestant religion, and when I say the Protestant religion, I mean the Church of England, as by law established'. In the latter half of the twentieth century (if not before), with globalization, that lesson has become obvious. 'Religion' can never now be seen as coterminous with Christianity, or any other single religion.

It is equally necessary, however, to recognise that 'religion' is not being restricted to any single *kind* among the religions, such as the 'world religions'. It refers to *religiosity*, in general, rather than to its expression in any particular form of religion, or even in any particular type of religion.

At this point, because 'religiosity' has only recently begun to be used by scholars without the opprobrium that it still has in ordinary speech, it is necessary to point out that neither religion nor religiosity implies a value judgement. In any particular case, they may be judged true or false, good or bad, helpful or harmful. However, as general categories, they are as neutral, ethically, as money or power, gender or sexuality.

Further, while they may be nearly as universal as those categories, there is no assumption (or hidden agenda) that this *must* be the case. General statements depend upon the meaning given to words. They may be indulged in, but, from the present point of view, rather as games to be played, than as utopia's, to be assumed, or aimed at, let alone imposed.

So the use of 'religion' is meant to be decidedly unemotional and low-key. If it causes offence in some context, then some other term, expressing as much as can be mutually agreed, may be more appropriate. Just as Tertullian *(sic)* said, that what mattered was to have the Christian thing done, rather than having it labelled as Christian; so, what matters in this field is communication, regarding the reality that is being apprehended, rather than the use of a particular label, if it hinders rather than helps communication and communion.

'Implicit Religion' a hypothesis

Protests about the use of the word 'religion' are less common in the 1990s than in the 1960s, in keeping with the general change from a modern society to a postmodern culture. When they do occur, they are usually expressed by someone who is out of touch with the contemporary meaning of 'religion'. While their sense of passion helps to provoke reflection (cp Durkheim and St Paul), that is not the main reason why the expression is retained, and the hypothesis of its usefulness continues to be maintained.

The expression is retained, because it reminds the student to try and place his or her study, methods and findings, within the overall and challenging context of the study of religion. Alternative expressions, such as 'ultimate concern(s)' or 'value(s) systems', may succeed in avoiding the *angst* aroused by the wider context of 'religion', but they lose the benefits to be gained from such an all-embracing frame of reference.

They also tend to concentrate upon a single aspect or form of the overall area, and hence become exclusivist or reductionist. 'Ultimate concern', for instance, may find a natural home within the context of student discussion groups, or 'value system', within the context of political think-tanks, but neither of them is indigenous within less philosophical or self-conscious contexts. The retention of 'religion', on the other hand, immediately raises such issues as ritual, and fellowship, for instance - without necessitating their interpretation either as mere means to other ends, or as ends in themselves.

The overall hypothesis (that we may gain in our understanding of some of the phenomena of secular life, if we compare them with what we already know about what we call religious life), continues to be maintained, then. There are several reasons for this, despite the offence it sometimes occasions.

On the one hand, it is, as has been said, a low-key approach. It is a hypothesis, with a hermeneutic aim, rather than a doctrine, with a dogmatic objective. In the same way, it is only suggested as one, possible, *additional* approach, to assist our overall understanding of people. Its concern with intentionality means that it is holistic. Yet it cannot and would not displace or replace any of the other human sciences - whose concerns are also, rightly, both specialist and holistic, but with different perspectives, from different points of view.

On the other hand, it can claim to be forwarding (and possibly completing) a process that began long ago, and is well established, but remains unfinished. This is a process that began with the application of civil law to the Church, and continued with the application of secular disciplines to the study of religion. Time was,

16

when the clergy, or the faithful, protested at such 'innovations' (or reinstatements).   Today, though, theologians and believers are amongst the first to explore the part played by 'non-theological' factors in church history or Church growth, or to insist that human rights are right (even within Churches) because they are human.

If two or three, or more, approaches are better than one, and two or more heads are better than one, why should this apply in the one direction and not in the other? If the double perspective, of both religious and secular approaches, furthers our understanding of the religious, by helping us to focus and 'place' it, why should the same not be true of the secular? Indeed, to deny the validity of the question, might suggest that it possesses (at least for the defenders of its inviolability) some kind of taboo, and so itself confirm the propriety of such exploration.

The popular use of 'religious'

There is, however, nothing new in the approach that is summed up in this way of using 'religion'. For the 'man-in-the-street' ('person-on-the-pavement'?) regularly uses 'religion' in precisely this way. He says, 'I read the papers religiously'; meaning, faithfully, ie regularly *and* carefully; habitually, but not compulsively; obsessively (if you like), yet also by deliberate choice.

He makes his meaning crystal clear, when he pronounces: She goes to church every week, but her real religion is her family (or, gossiping, or whatever). Thus 'religion' is already generally understood, outside the intelligentsia, and at least in England, in terms of the practice of core intention(s).

To maintain the implicit-religion hypothesis, then, and to retain 'religion' in its description, opens up the possibility both of a wider public understanding and dialogue, as well as cross-fertilisation with what has become known as 'religious studies'. While there is no desire to impose the use of 'religion' upon any who do not wish it, neither is there felt to be any ultimate obligation to avoid its use altogether. There is room for both the majority and minority view; neither of them should be understood as sectarian.

17

The significance of 'implicit'

The adjectival (or adverbial) qualifier, *implicit* (or *implicitly*), is (like *religion*) not without the disadvantages of ambiguity. For it is not immediately apparent whether the evidence itself is implicit or its religiosity. In fact, it doesn't necessarily refer to either.

Thus, an individual or group may be vociferous, and the philosophy thus articulated could still be seen as evidence of their implicit religion. Furthermore, they themselves might even see that philosophy as being in some way a religious statement; for instance, it might take the form of one of the recognised religious creeds. Yet it could still be seen as evidence of their implicit religion. For the criterion of *implicit* religion is not a simple negative, such as a lack of articulation (verbal or otherwise), or the absence of an explicitly religious frame of reference. It is positive: the presence of commitment, *of any kind*.

Thus implicit religion is not necessarily in opposition to explicit religion. Yet neither does it necessarily support or develop into one of the explicit religions; any more than it necessarily owes its origin to one of the recognised religions. The concept is innocent of theory, as well as neutral in value.

Some of the reasons for choosing this expression appeared in the course of discussing the drawbacks that accompany any choice of expression, but in this case they were particularly connected with the emotive quality of the noun and the imprecision of the adjective. Thus it has been suggested that it has the advantages that come from drawing upon a fairly clear (and widespread) core of meaning, by using that noun. Yet, by its adjective, it demarcates (with reasonable success) a particular, and (among *literati*) somewhat novel, application of the concept.

In time, however, the adjective could become redundant. In other words, some kind of religiosity could be seen as a natural and inevitable dimension of any kind of secularity. So formal Religious Studies might automatically include its study within their concerns.

This could be seen as part of a continuing process which (from a western perspective) has already broadened out from the study of Christianity, to the study, not only of the other monotheistic Semitic traditions, but to 'polytheistic' and even a-theistic traditions, such as Hinayana Buddhism, and including traditions in small-scale societies that 'did not so much as know' they had 'a religion'. It is, likewise, part of a process that has 'deepened', from the comparison of texts (within a single tradition or across many), to the con-textualisation of both verbal and non-verbal 'texts' within, increasingly, every kind of system or charisma, from the political to the psychic.

There are signs, indeed, that this (final?) stage, of a long process, is already under way. On the one hand, the human sciences seem to be increasingly moving in this direction themselves. Not only are they increasingly concerned with the kind of areas with which religious studies has been concerned (world-view, ethics, identity, etc); they increasingly seem to feel that religious concepts provide the most appropriate terminology in which to discuss them (myth, ritual, charisma, etc). And, on the other hand, in the 1970s, if not in present circumstances, there were indeed Departments of Religious Studies, particularly in the United States, that included courses on civil (as against canonical) religion, and 'religion without the capital' (as against 'the Religions', with the capital letter) in their standard, introductory curricula.

So the time may not be too distant, when the study of the religions, during these last two centuries, begins to look like the Victorian fondness for collecting and classifying, abstracting and analysing, listing and labelling, museum-pieces. Some such de-construction may be the inevitable price of all description. The resulting morphology can serve, however, as a typology. Having changed the religious situation in India, for instance, by inventing the concept of 'Hindu-ism', it then becomes possible to see similarly 'Hindu' characteristics within the religions of other groups or individuals. However, for a host of reasons, the tendency is already to move back from the -isms, and refer to the religions of, or the religious traditions of, or the religious situation in, a geographical region, such as India or South Asia or wherever.

Again, the move away from such a 'fundamentalist' approach to our own categories, may be the harbinger of a much wider process. It may be described as a preference for starting with the empirical data (which we now have conceptual tools to help us discover), rather than with the (idealised) systems of ideas. It may be compared with making the bricks, with which to build a wall, as against searching for items to fit a blue-print. Should we end up building another set of store-rooms, at least they should be locally recognisable. Meanwhile, the concept of 'implicit religion', with the distinctive emphasis that is supplied by the addition of the adjective, seems to be necessary, to redress the balance by now pointing to the converse of explicit religion.

3 WHAT DOES 'IMPLICIT RELIGION' MEAN?

Resumé

The first chapter suggested that apprehending the reality, or intuiting what that reality would feel like if we could share its apprehension, requires a sympathetic imagination, in order to raise awareness of one's own experience and to search for echoes in it of what is being described. It may be compared to reading poetry.

The second chapter showed that naming the reality that is apprehended in this way is less difficult. We search for a form of words that will effectively communicate as much as possible of what is essential and lead to as little misunderstanding as possible.

Defining the terms used in that name is less easy, but is the task of this chapter. For we are back with the problem of trying to describe, at a fairly straightforward level of communication, the core of that which has been apprehended existentially.

The needle in the haystack

In the case of 'implicit religion', this difficulty is compounded by our desire to leave open-ended the specific content of that which is apprehended. We could say that we are looking less for a noun than an adjective or adverb, less for a 'what', than for a 'how'. Like the proverbial needle in the haystack, we are unlikely to distinguish it from its surroundings, until it pricks us.

This problem is, of course, not unique to 'implicit religion'. Religious studies have similar difficulty in defining *religion*. As Ugo Bianchi (*The History of Religion*, Leiden: E.J. Brill, 1975:201f) says, until we have found what we are looking for, we cannot be quite sure what the 'religion' we are looking for, looks like! (We have more idea, of what it *feels* like.) However, the same problem occurs in other spheres. The engineer will say of the dam that has collapsed, or the car that won't start, We can't know what the problem is, until we've put it right. (Economists and politicians might feel the same.)

A definition of implicit religion, therefore, is by no means intended to describe the content of the implicit religion that is present in any particular situation. It will *not* say, for instance, 'Religion' consists of beliefs and rituals and fellowships, and therefore we are simply searching for their secular parallels. These

21

may be pointers, raising questions that should be asked; but, with implicit religion as with religion, we may miss the heart of what we are seeking, if we only use the existing lenses in order to find parallels. It may be possible to *translate* a specific implicit religion into such terms, but we will need to remember that it is a translation.

The motive power, with which we are concerned, may be an existential response; it may be described by its owner(s) in terms of what they feel to be a truth; but to then suggest that they do so 'because' they thus believe, might well be to mistake our interpretation for their reality. It would put the cart (of myth) before the horse (of ritual), both as a report of their self-description, and as an explanation of their behaviour.

Defining implicit religion is a way of laying down the parameters within which, whatever is found, will fall. As we reflect upon behaviour (in the broadest sense), or hit upon an explanation for some particular aspect of it, the description of the reality pointed to by this attempt to describe it, will serve as guide-lines. Applying them, we may decide that the explanation is (for instance), psychological rather than implicit-religious. We may then tentatively conclude that a further, implicit-religious understanding either is, or is not, possible.

Three definitions

Three definitions of implicit religion may, then, be suggested. They are three descriptions of the general reality that has been apprehended, and to which each expression tries to point. Their plurality may suggest a lack of clarity or of decisiveness. Certainly, all three have been worked with for over a quarter of a century without any preference emerging. However, it might therefore also be suggested, that, far from indicating conceptual uncertainty, their plurality demonstrates phenomenal certitude. Their number, and hence relativity, witness to the absoluteness of that which is apprehended. It is a fact of experience, before it is a logical construct.

The first of these definitions is, Commitments. If, in its turn, we look to the Oxford English Dictionary for definitions of 'commitment', we find a certain paucity of description, (Rodney J Hunter, in *Implicit Religion: Journal of the Centre for the Study of*

22

Implicit Religion and Contemporary Spirituality, vol II, 1999, shows how the gap might be filled.) This may illustrate something of the character of what the word means: we know its reality, but find it difficult to put into words.

It points to behaviour whose explanation involves, in part, the exercise of a certain freedom. Fortunately the term does not suggest a restriction to self-conscious and deliberately willed, individual decisions. Commitments can be inherited with one's mother's milk, and be entirely unconscious, unknown even to their owner, until perhaps brought to the surface by an individual or national moment of crisis (literally, a 'judgement', ie a 'revelation; - of what we are like, and are). This expression, therefore, not only seems to fit with what it is intended to describe, but has the additional merit of acknowledging the validity of the age-old problem of free will, without suggesting any particular position regarding its extent.

A second definition is, Integrating foci. This one lacks the extreme 'portability' of the first, but may appear somewhat less intuitive and more conceptual, because it provides a point of intersection between its two components. It suggests that 'implicit religion' will reveal itself in those focal points that integrate wider areas of life.

Apart from its apparent suitability, in describing what is apprehended as being 'implicitly religious', *integrating foci* has the additional advantage of suggesting that it could refer to either individuals or to groups. This ambiguity of reference is intentional, for 'implicit religion' (like 'religion') is meant to span the whole gamut of the area in which the human operates. Just as 'commitment' seems able to suggest (without the need for *ad hoc* extension) that it is concerned with any and every level of human consciousness, from the subconscious and the unconscious, through the conscious and self-conscious, to the 'sur-conscious', so 'integrating foci' seems to suggest, by its natural and unvarnished self, every width and depth of human interaction, from the individual and personal, through the familial and face-to-face, to the social, societal, corporate, and species.

The third definition is, Intensive concerns with extensive effects. This cannot so easily be popped into a sentence in place of that which it purports to copy, but it gains in memorability from its internal contrast and 'rhyme'. As it happens, it follows closely, if not exactly, the definition of religion itself, that was suggested by F B Welbourn, the Africanist (and, perhaps not altogether coincidentally, Anglican).

Apart from its inherent aptitude for the task of describing the object apprehended, this definition likewise has the merit of excluding a potential restriction of reference, and suggesting the reunification of distinctions that have heuristic value, but run the risk of artificially compartmentalising reality. For it spells out, what is implied by its predecessors, that, no matter how passionate the concern, its relevance, from the point of view of implicit religion, also requires a breadth of reference.

Thus a brief experience of ecstasy, on the part of an individual or a group, whether unique or occurring repeatedly, or the most deep-seated and unconscious assumption or prejudice, either solitary or societal, will be of psychological or sociological or anthropological concern, rather than implicit-religious interest, so long as it appears isolated from the remainder of experience. In this way it ensures that the distinctions between the sacred and the secular, the holy and the profane, the special and the ordinary, between religion and the rest of life, are both acknowledged as necessary and accurate and helpful, and yet simultaneously restored to reciprocal relationship. It does for 'religion' what the other two definitions did for the individual and society, and for the conscious and unconscious: it spans a spectrum.

Comm ct

As it happens, a fourth 'definition', or description (or paraphrase, or synonym) has occasionally come to mind: 'human depths' (Douglas J. Davies, *Implicit Religion, journal of the Centre for the Study of Implicit Religion and Contemporary Spirituality*, vol I, 1998). It has seemed appropriate and accurate, but has not been worked with, perhaps because each of its terms is more difficult to explain, and potentially harder to agree upon, than those which have been used.

As it also happened, these three definitions were each spontaneously used in turn, in the trio of empirical studies that were undertaken to test the viability of this approach and concept. However, before reporting those three applications of the concept, it will help to grasp its meaning if we bring together two other terms ('civil religion' and 'invisible religion') that point to this same reality; and mention two other terms ('folk religion' and 'popular religion') that are sometimes uncritically linked with it.

[Handwritten notes:]

Individual
Conscious / unconscious — commitment

Societal
Intuitive / conceptual — integrating
foci

Spans a spectrum
Sacred / secular   Intensive awareness
holy / profane   accurate /
special / ordinary   helpful /   extensive effects
religion / earth   restored to
          reciprocal
          relationship.

4   WHAT IS CLOSEST TO IMPLICIT RELIGION?

Twenty-plus years ago, it was possible for a single student to compile a list of some fifty terms that he had come across that referred to something like implicit religion. The list showed how many people, when considering society as a whole, let alone individual experiences, had had a similar apprehension. However, it also showed that very few of the terms were as impartial (and therefore available for open-ended research or teaching) as 'implicit religion', as that is used here. They also hardly ever cited any empirical observation to illustrate their meaning - although a number urged the necessity and importance of such studies.

Since then, another such list could probably have been compiled. It could have included a contribution from a student of the 'inherent' religion of the *Sun* newspaper; or the 'innate' religion, reported by a colleague from a discussion on the Moscow underground; or the 'incipient religion' to which one colleague keeps referring. One such list, though, seemed enough to make the point. Instead, therefore, a handful that are frequently used, and sometimes thought to be the same as implicit religion, can be mentioned and compared/contrasted with it.

'Civil religion'

'Civil religion' has already been mentioned.   The expression originates with Rousseau. Writing after the post-Reformation wars of religion in western Europe, Rousseau was well aware of the dangers of (national) religion(s), but felt that some 'minimal religion' was necessary to society. His ideal creed, therefore, included belief in a supreme God, in the punishment of vice after death, and in tolerance of different opinions in this life.

The phrase sprang to fame, especially among United States students of religion, following an essay in 1966 on *Civil Religion in America*, by Robert Bellah, an American sociologist, who had studied the Tokugawa religion in (or, perhaps better, of) Japan. Indeed, the expression became somewhat notorious, for it was sometimes supposed, firstly, that Bellah simply saw American nationalism as the country's civil religion, and secondly, that he endorsed it. This misunderstanding was fuelled by the tendency

26

to confuse the actual constitutional principle of the separation of Church and State, with an abstract theory regarding the desirability of a putative divorce between religion and society. In the event however, the issue was ignited by the then current controversy over the Vietnamese War.

In fact, the essay was brief, careful, cautious, and critical. A few passages may suggest that it could be something of a model. It begins:

> While some have argued that Christianity is the national faith, and others that church and synagogue celebrate only the generalized religion of 'the American Way of Life', few have realized that there actually exists alongside of and rather clearly differentiated from the churches an elaborate and well institutionalized civil religion in America. This article argues not only that there is such a thing, but also that this religion - or perhaps better, this religious dimension - has its own seriousness and integrity and requires the same care in understanding that any other religion does ...
>
> Why something so obvious should have escaped serious analytical attention is in itself an interesting problem. Part of the reason is probably the controversial nature of the subject. From the earliest years of the nineteenth century, conservative religious and political groups have argued that Christianity is, in fact, the national religion. Some of them have from time to time and as recently as the 1950s proposed constitutional amendments that would explicitly recognise the sovereignty of Christ ...
>
> In defending the doctrine of separation of church and state, opponents of such groups have denied that the national polity has, intrinsically, anything to do with religion at all. The moderates on this issue have insisted that the American state has taken a permissive and indeed supportive attitude toward religious groups (tax exemption etc.), thus favoring religion but still missing the positive institutionalization with which I am concerned. But part of the reason this issue has been left in obscurity is certainly due to the peculiarly western concept of 'religion' as

27

denoting a single type of collectivity of which an individual can be a member of one and only one at a time. The Durkheimian notion that every group has a religious dimension, which would be seen as obvious in southern or eastern Asia, is foreign to us. This obscures the recognition of such dimensions in our society ...

The words and acts of the founding fathers, especially the first few presidents, shaped the form and tone of the civil religion as it has been maintained ever since. Though much is selectively derived from Christianity, this religion is clearly not itself Christianity. For one thing, neither Washington nor Adams nor Jefferson mentions Christ in his inaugural address; nor do any of the subsequent presidents, although not one of them fails to mention God ...

The God of the civil religion is not only rather 'unitarian', he is also on the austere side, much more related to order, law, and right than to salvation and love. Even though he is somewhat deist in cast, he is by no means simply a watchmaker God. He is actively interested and involved in history, with a special concern for America. Here the analogy has much less to do with natural law than with ancient Israel; the equation of America with Israel in the idea of the 'American Israel' is not infrequent ...

What we have, then, from the earliest years of the republic is a collection of beliefs, symbols, and rituals with respect to sacred things and institutionalized in a collectivity. This religion - there seems no other word for it - while not antithetical to, and indeed sharing much in common with, Christianity was neither sectarian nor in any specific sense Christian. At a time when the society was overwhelmingly Christian, it seems unlikely that this lack of Christian reference was meant to spare the feelings of the tiny nonchristian minority. Rather, the civil religion expressed what those who set the precedents felt was appropriate under the circumstances. It reflected their private as well as public views. Nor was the civil religion simply 'religion in general'. While generality was undoubtedly seen as a virtue by some, the civil religion was specific enough when it came to the topic of America. Precisely because of this specificity, the civil religion was saved from empty formalism and served as a genuine vehicle of natural religious self-understanding.

He then begins an exercise in 'comparative religion', by placing this civil religion alongside historical Christianity.

...There was an implicit but quite clear division of function between the civil religion and Christianity. Under the doctrine of religious liberty, an exceptionally wide sphere of personal piety and voluntary social action was left to the churches. But the churches were neither to control the state nor to be controlled by it. The national magistrate, whatever his private religious views, operates under the rubrics of the civil religion as long as he is in his official capacity, as we had already seen in the case of Kennedy. This accommodation was undoubtedly the product of a particular historical moment and of a cultural background dominated by Protestantism of several varieties and by the Enlightenment, but it has survived despite subsequent changes in the cultural and religious climate ...

...I would argue that the civil religion at its best is a genuine apprehension of universal and transcendent religious reality as seen in or, one could almost say, as revealed through the experience of the American people. Like all religions, it has suffered various deformations and demonic distortions. At its best, it has been neither so general that it has lacked incisive relevance to the American scene nor so particular that it has placed American society above universal human values ...

Perhaps the real animus of the religious critics has been not so much against the civil religion in itself but against its pervasive and dominating influence within the sphere of church religion ...

Finally, Bellah turns to developments that were taking place, or might take place, within this civil religion.

The civil religion is obviously involved in the most pressing moral and political issues of the day. But it is also caught in another kind of crisis, theoretical and theological, of which it is at the moment largely unaware. 'God' has clearly been a central symbol in the civil religion from the beginning and remains so today. This symbol is just as central to the civil religion as it is to Judaism or Christianity. In the late eighteenth century this posed no problem; even Tom Paine, contrary to his detractors, was not an atheist. From left to right, and regardless of church or sect, all could accept the idea of God. But today the meaning of the word 'God' is by no means so clear or so obvious. There is no formal creed in the civil religion. We have had a Catholic president; it is conceivable that we could have a Jewish one. But could we have an agnostic president? Could a man with conscientious scruples about using the word 'God' the way Kennedy and Johnson have used it be elected chief magistrate of our country? If the whole God symbolism requires reformation there will be obvious consequences for the civil religion, consequences perhaps of liberal alienation and of fundamentalist ossification that have not so far been prominent in this realm. The civil religion has been a point of articulation between the profoundest commitments of the Western religious and philosophical tradition and the common beliefs of ordinary Americans. It is not too soon to consider how the deepening theological crisis may affect the future of this articulation.

...[T]he emergence of a genuine transnational sovereignty would certainly change this. It would necessitate the incorporation of vital international symbolism into our civil religion, or, perhaps a better way of putting it, it would result in American civil religion's becoming simply a part of a new civil religion of the world. It is useless [?] to speculate on the form such a civil religion might take, though it obviously would draw on religious traditions beyond the sphere of biblical religion alone. Fortunately, since the American civil religion is not the worship of the American nation but an understanding of the American experience in the light of ultimate and universal reality, the reorganisation entailed by such a new situation need not disrupt the American civil religion's continuity. A world civil religion could be accepted as a fulfillment and not a denial of American civil religion. Indeed, such an outcome has been the eschatological hope of American civil religion from the beginning ...

Behind the civil religion at every point lie biblical archetypes: Exodus, Chosen People, Promised Land, New Jerusalem, Sacrificial Death, and Rebirth. But the civil religion is also genuinely American and genuinely new. It has its own prophets and its own martyrs, its own sacred events and sacred places, its own solemn rituals and symbols. It is concerned that America be a society as perfectly in accord with the will of God as men can make it and a light to all the nations ...

...It is in need - as is any living faith - of continual reformation, of being measured by universal standards. But it is not evident that our civil religion is incapable of growth and new insight.

Less famous, but equally exemplary, is M P Nilsson's *History of Greek Religion*, 1925. His chapters on 'civic religion' start at the other end of the spectrum from Presidential Inaugural Addresses: they describe festivals and soothsaying, from the point of view of social class, cultural context, and religious expression.

Both ends, of each of these three spectra, are necessary for a complete picture of the (implicit, or otherwise) religion of a society. It may, however, help to portray the whole spectrum if we exploit the existence of two terms in English to translate the French *civile* (or the German *Zivil*). Thus, 'civic' can describe the formal and societal, and 'civil' the informal and general. (Both Bellah, and Nilsson's translators, unfortunately transpose them!) Together, however, they cover the social aspect of implicit religion.

31

'Popular religion'

Civil religion, then, if it be of the sort described by Nilsson as 'civic', largely overlaps with 'popular religion'. This term tends to be used in connection with warmer climates, where people live closer together, sometimes in Third World conditions. Typically it refers to local versions of global traditions, in which initiative tends to lie with (religiously-speaking) non-specialists, even when the specialists, and their tradition's symbols, are used. It is easily photographed when it takes the form of an urban festival or a pilgrimage to a shrine. However, the term is also used when close-knit rural peasantries gather together, or when they act religiously to meet practical, individual or familial needs in this world.

Popular religion would seem to disappear, at least from sight, in societies that have been marked by secularisation. However, that could be little more than a tautology. Perhaps it would be more helpful to say that popular religion tends to disappear with the growth of domesticity, individualism, privacy, privatisation, atomisation, and *anomie*. Its demise is part of the loss of popular culture, and of any public culture.

Yet in other forms popular religion may survive. It may indeed be public, but without being communal. It can be commonly practiced, without being practiced in common. It could take secular forms. The *sacrifices*, of effort, time and resources, that are put into Christmas shopping, or holiday travel, for instance, suggest that this may be the case. Some may feel that the analogy is necessary, in order to make sense of such behaviour. So the study of implicit religion at a social level, may be, in part, the study of the 'popular religion' of 'secular' societies. The mundane characteristics of such activities by no means rules out their simultaneous religiosity.

'Folk religion'

In Britain, 'folk religion' is often associated with 'implicit religion'. The expression began to be used in the 1970s, especially by Church of England clergy, to refer to ways in which people 'made use of' the Church (its buildings, ceremonies, personnel), especially for the *rites de passages*. As the attitude was invariably pejorative, its equation with 'implicit religion' was doubly unfortunate, as the latter strove, above all, to be non-judgemental.

The concept of 'folk religion' did, however, begin to acknowledge that such occasions contained some kind of religious significance. Its users may have assumed that 'Occasional Offices' were somehow casual (until a refusal revealed the depth of feeling that they marshall), rather than making and marking an Occasion. They may also have tried to judge commitment, by visible and repeated action. Yet at least it opened up the possibility of understanding such behaviour in terms of implicit religion, instead of (for instance) airily dismissing the desire for Christenings as an additional 'inoculation', against bad luck in this life or divine disfavour in the next. In fact, though, the pejorative air displayed in using the term, was sometimes probably a ploy to get a hearing. Certainly, today the ecclesiastical attitude towards such occasional expressions of the religious (as in the 1997 response to the death of the Princess of Wales) is increasingly neutral, or positively sympathetic (albeit sometime mystified).

Clearly, what is called folk religion in this country, is one, relatively popular, expression of implicit religion. The same phrase is used in Northern Europe, however, with rather a different meaning. There it draws upon the 'folk memory', of the barbarian (*Volk*) invasions, and the tribe's collective conversion to Christianity, in the first millennium of the current era. In that sense, 'folk religion' is more corporate and societal, and, in terms of regular worship for instance, even less often expressed in direct liturgical participation than in Britain.

In Japan, 'folk religion' is used differently again. There it refers (with an attractive lack of judgement) to that congeries of individual and familial practices that are seen as necessary to the development and survival of the greater traditions. This use obviously overlaps with one end of the 'popular religion' spectrum elsewhere.

'Invisible religion'
Last, but by no means least, of the terms with which 'implicit religion' is often associated, is 'invisible religion'. Luckmann's short work of that name, appeared in its final form in 1967, a year after Bellah's essay. It contains something of a theory of religion in general, and very little by way of empirical observation. In those

respects it almost exactly reverses the position of implicit religion (in this context). In the current case, it was empirical observation that gave rise to reflection on religion in general (see chapters 8-10), whereas Luckmann has only recently begun to apply his theory. There is little if any difference between the two concepts, other than the sense faculty which they make typological. However, speech, as a metaphor, seems a little less paradoxical than sight, and so has been retained by the present student.

As with Bellah's essay, some quotations may provide a flavour of this, the best-known theoretical underpinning for the present concept.

We may begin, however, as he begins, by quoting from William James, *The Varieties of Religious Experience*:

> As there thus seems to be no one elementary religious emotion, but only a common storehouse of emotion upon which religious objects may draw, so there might conceivably also prove to be no one specific and essential kind of religious object, and no one specific and essential kind of religious act.

In other words, the adjective *religious* may often prove accurate, while the noun *religion* may lead us into confusion.

Thus, Luckmann begins by suggesting that 'the central question of the sociology of religion ... is, at the same time, an important problem for sociological theory as a whole: What are the conditions under which transcendent, superordinated and integrating structures of meaning are socially objectivated?' (1967:26). He goes on to say that the

> survival of traditional forms of church religion, the absence, in the West, of an institutionalized antichurch, and the overwhelming significance of Christianity in the shaping of the modern western world have combined in obscuring the possibility that a new religion is in the making. It is this possibility that we shall try to raise from a purely speculative status to the status of a productive hypothesis in the sociological theory of religion (1967:40).

He then introduces what he calls 'the anthropological condition of religion', which is minimalist, functional, and species-wide. Thus:

Detachment from immediate experience originates in the confrontation with fellow men in the face-to-face situation. It leads to the individuation of consciousness and permits the construction of interpretive schemes, ultimately, of systems of meaning. Detachment from immediate experience finds its complement in the integration of past, present and future into a socially defined, morally relevant biography. This integration develops in continuous social relations and leads to the formation of consciences. The individuation of the two complementary aspects of Self occurs in social processes. The organism - in isolation nothing but a separate pole of 'meaningless' subjective processes - becomes a Self by embarking with others upon the construction of an 'objective' and moral universe of meaning. Thereby the organism transcends its biological nature.

It is in keeping with an elementary sense of the concept of religion to call the transcendence of biological nature by the human organism a religious phenomenon ... [which] rests upon the functional relation of Self and society. We may, therefore, regard the social processes that lead to the formation of Self as fundamentally religious. This view, incidentally, does no violence to the etymology of the term. It may be objected from a theological and 'substantivist' position on religion that in this view religion becomes an all-encompassing phenomenon. We suggest that this is not a valid objection. The transcendence of biological nature *is* a universal phenomenon of mankind. Another objection is to be taken more seriously. It may be said that calling the processes that lead to the formation of Self religious does, perhaps, avoid a sociologistic identification of society and religion but also fails to provide a specific account of the 'objective' and institutional forms of religion in society. We plead guilty to this charge. The analysis so far [N.B.] did no more than identify the general source from which spring the historically differentiated social forms of religion. We would contend, however, that this represents a necessary first step in the sociological theory of religion. In showing the religious quality of the social processes by which consciousness and conscience are individuated we identified the universal yet specific anthropological condition of religion (1967:48-9).

He then discussed 'the social forms of religion':

Institutional specialization as a *social form of religion* ... is characterized by standardization of the sacred cosmos in a well-defined doctrine, differentiation of full-time religious roles, transfer of sanctions enforcing doctrinal and ritual conformity to special agencies and the emergence of organizations of the 'ecclesiastic' type. [Such] institutional specialization of religion always contains the possibility of an antithesis between 'religion' and 'society' ... [I]n all societies characterized by this social form of religion ... the segregation of the sacred cosmos in the world view is matched, to some extent, by specialization of religious roles in the social structure and by the existence of groups claiming a distinctly religious quality (1967:66-8).

Uniting the 'anthropological condition' of religion and the 'social forms' of religion, he describes 'individual religiosity'.

Religion is rooted in a basic anthropological fact: the transcendence of biological nature by human organisms. The individual human potential for transcendence is realized, originally, in social processes that rest on the reciprocity of face-to-face situations. These processes lead to the construction of objective world views, the articulation of sacred universes and, under certain circumstances, to institutional specialization of religion. The social forms of religion are thus based on what is, in a certain sense, an individual religious phenomenon: the individuation of consciousness and conscience in the matrix of human inter-subjectivity.

The concrete historical individual, of course, does not go about constructing world views and sacred universes. He is born into a pre-existing society and into a prefabricated world view. He does not therefore achieve the status of a human person in genuinely original acts of transcendence. Humanity, as a reality that transcends biological nature, is pre-established for him in the social forms of religion. The individuation of consciousness and conscience of historical individuals is objectively determined by historical religions in one of their social forms.

[T]he individuation of consciousness and conscience occurs for historical individuals in the internalization of an already constructed world view rather than in the original creation of world views. The world view with its underlying hierarchy of significance becomes an individual system of relevance that is superimposed on the stream of consciousness. It is a constitutive element of personal identity. The personal identity of an historical individual is thus, the subjective expression of the objective significance of a world view. Earlier we defined the world view as a universal social form of religion. Correspondingly, we may now define personal identity as a universal form of individual religiosity (1967:69-70).

Summarising his position, he prepares to launch into a catena of questions that are of primary concern in this context.

The anthropological condition of religion is to be found in the 'dialectics' of individual and society that pervade the processes in which consciousness and conscience are individuated. These processes lead to the objectivation of a world view which functions as a 'transcendent' hierarchy of meaning *vis-a-vis* the immanently 'unbound' subjective stream of consciousness. We defined, therefore, the world view as a universal but non-specific social form of religion. Its subjective correlate is to be found in the internalized system of relevance which forms the basis of a personal identity. Our analysis

37

uncovered the conditions under which specific social forms of religion emerge from that universal form. In the universal form the religious function is diffused in society. It is increasingly concentrated in the specific social forms which range from an articulation of a sacred cosmos in the world view to full institutional specialization of religion. The subjective correlate of the former is to be found in the internal segregation of religious representations in the form of an individual system of 'ultimate' relevance. The subjective correlate of the latter is to be found in the configuration of internalized dimensions of the 'official' model of religion, a configuration which we called church-oriented religiosity.

An objective world view is, of course, a constitutive element of any society, just as an individual system of relevance is a constitutive element of personal identity. The statement that religion is present in non-specific form in all societies and all 'normal' (socialized) individuals is, therefore, axiomatic. It specifies a religious dimension in the 'definition' of individual and society but is empty of specific empirical content (1967:78).

So, turning to contemporary society, he suggests:
What are usually taken as symptoms of the decline of traditional Christianity may be symptoms of a more revolutionary change: the replacement of the institutional specialization of religion by a new social form of religion.

One thing we may assert with confidence: The norms of traditional religious institutions - as congealed in an 'official' or formerly 'official' model of religion - cannot serve as a yardstick for assessing religion in contemporary society. Before we can arrive at an understanding of religion in modern society, we must, at least, ask the right questions. It was the purpose of our theoretical analysis of the social forms of religion to provide the criteria for deciding what are these questions. What is the hierarchy of significance in the world views of contemporary industrial societies? Is that hierarchy articulated in a sacred cosmos? What is their basis in the social structure? Are they located in an institutional area that 'specializes' in religion? Or are the religious representations distributed over several institutional areas? In other words, can we consider modern religion to be 'regressing' to a social form of religion that preceded institutional specialization? Or does the sacred cosmos in modern society have an institutional basis at all? If not, how is the sacred cosmos objectivated in society? - that is, in what way is it part of an objective social reality? What role do the traditional institutions that 'specialized' in religion play in this context?

It may be useful, furthermore, to reformulate these questions so as to address them to the corresponding phenomena on the social-psychological level. What are the norms that determine the effective priorities in the everyday lives of typical members of modern industrial societies? What are the subjective relevance systems that have an overarching, sense-integrating function in contemporary life? How clearly are they articulated in individual systems of 'ultimate' significance? How are they linked to social roles and positions? To what extent is the traditional 'official' model of religion still being internalized and what is its relation to the prevalent systems of 'ultimate' significance? (1967:90-1).

In the absence, he says, of the necessary sensitive and sustained research, he tries to sketch some of the characteristics and themes of the new social (or perhaps better, 'cultural') form of religion that is emerging. Thus:

The social form of religion emerging in modern industrial societies is characterized by the direct accessibility of an assortment of religious representations to potential consumers. The sacred cosmos is mediated neither through a specialized domain of religious institutions nor through other primary public institutions. It is the direct accessibility of the sacred cosmos, more precisely, of an assortment of religious themes, which makes religion today essentially a phenomenon of the 'private sphere'. The emerging social form of religion thus differs significantly from older social forms of religion which were characterized either by the diffusion of the sacred cosmos through the institutional structure of society or through institutional specialization of religion.

The appearance of secondary institutions supplying the market for 'ultimate' significance does not mean that the sacred cosmos - after a period of institutional specialization - is once again diffused through the social structure. The decisive difference is that the primary public institutions do not maintain the sacred cosmos [or *vice versa*, as they are 'autonomous']; they merely regulate the legal and economic frame within which occurs the competition on the 'ultimate' significance market. Furthermore, diffusion of the sacred cosmos through the social structure characterizes societies in which the 'private sphere', in the strict sense of the term, does not exist and in which the distinction between primary and secondary institutions is meaningless.

The continuous dependence of the secondary institutions on consumer preference and, thus, on the 'private sphere' makes it very unlikely that the social objectivation of themes originating in the 'private sphere' and catering to it will eventually lead to the articulation of a consistent and closed sacred cosmos and the specialization, once again, of religious institutions. This is one of the several reasons that justify the assumption that we are not merely describing an interregnum between the extinction of one 'official' model and the appearance of a new one, but, rather, that we are observing the emergence of a new social form of religion characterized neither by diffusion of the sacred cosmos through the social structure nor by institutional specialization of religion .... [T]he prevalent individual systems of 'ultimate' significance will consist of a loose and rather unstable hierarchy of 'opinions' legitimating the affectively determined priorities of 'private' life (103-5).

He suggests some of these (related) 'modern religious themes'. They are: individual autonomy, and hence self-expression and self-realization, and, somewhat paradoxically - but as an extension of the private sphere - familism.

It may be said, in sum, that the modern sacred cosmos symbolizes the social-historical phenomenon of individualism and that it bestows, in various articulations, 'ultimate' significance upon the structurally determined phenomenon of the 'private sphere'. We [have] tried to show that the structure of the modern sacred cosmos and its thematic content represent the emergence of a new social form of religion which, in turn, is determined by a radical transformation in the relation of the individual to the social order.

How it began —
Secular religion.

ITS APPLICATION

5 IMPLICIT RELIGION: IN INDIVIUALS

In 1968, having been a curate in a parish and a chaplain in a school, I found that no one was studying what I (at first) called 'secular religion'. Meeting F B Welbourn (who had long urged its study), I began to read in the field of religious and social studies, with a view to testing the concept's viability. If it proved useful to me, it might also be of interest to others, so as a precaution I also enrolled for a formal qualification.

Subsequently an academic conference has been held each year since 1978, and, since 1983, an annual short course in Religious Education as well as three study days for clergy and other churchpeople. The charitable status of these activities was recognised by the formation of the Network for the Study of Implicit Religion, in 1985. The original wish, to see them professionally focussed, was advanced in 1997 when the recently formed Centre for the Study of Implicit Religion and Contemporary Spirituality was located at Middlesex University.

That is to anticipate the unfolding of the story, but there are advantages in describing the stages as they have occurred so far, for the study of implicit religion is in many ways still in its infancy. Neither its recognition nor its study, neither its conceptualisation nor its methodology, have emerged full-grown from anyone's side. It has, however, progressed from being a non-subject, in the 1960s. Clergy and teachers have likewise considered it suitable for their on-going professional education.

The interviews

This is, indeed, how it began. For my first thought was to talk - or rather, to listen - to individuals, to try and find out 'what made them tick'. My first care, however, was to avoid simply looking for parallels to what is associated with the Christian religion, or any other religion. I did not, therefore, start with any list of the ingredients that go to make up either a particular religion, or of religion in general. As a result of not even checking my questions against any such a list, however, I realised when I had finished my hundred interviews, that I had omitted any sustained attempt to discover people's experiences of fellowship. (In reporting the

44

interviews, I therefore appended a list of questions that might have been asked to elicit information in this area, as well as a number of other questions, that might also have been used.)

In order to open up 'discussion' (talk, by the interviewees, in fact) of the kind of material I was looking for, I turned in the first place to the kind of statement that people make when they are summing up part of their 'philosophy of life', and converted such ruminations into questions. So I began by asking, What do you enjoy most in life?; and continued, at various points, What's the most important thing you do each year? week? day?; What makes an ordinary day into a really good day?; Is there any part of life that you'd really miss, if it was abolished? Do you think the world is changing for the better or the worse?; What do you think is the biggest problem in the world?; What's the most important job in the world?; and I concluded, Who are you? In the same vein, was a question about proverbs: Are there any that you really agree, or disagree, with?

In the second place, I used various games that people play, by asking, If you won a lot of money on the pools, What would you do with it?; or, If you had three wishes (and one of them had to be used on yourself), what would you wish for?; or, If you could change any one thing in the world, what would you change? I also invented a little game, which I used twice in the interview: Supposing a fifteen-year old, who can understand what you say but hasn't yet had your experience of life, asked you how he/she could tell right from wrong, what would you say?; and, If you had a minute to tell them your philosophy of life, what would you say?

A third group of questions may be said to have drawn upon a fairly simple version of Christianity, or of religion in general: What would a perfect world be like?; Who is most likely ever to put the world right? Do you think the world will ever be perfect?; and, What would a perfect person be like? As it happens, this last question was the only one, out of fifty, that 'failed', inasmuch as the answers were so clearly negative; yet the reasons they gave, made them not only instructive, but also revealing of those general outlooks, which constituted the object of the search.

A fourth type of question invited discourse about feelings: Is there anything that 'gets you', whether angry, or happy?; Is there anything that people do and you wish they didn't?; Is there anything you're afraid of?; Have you ever had any embarrassing experiences? If you were prepared to die for anything, what might it be?; Is there anything you really believe in, or don't believe in?

The last apparent 'series', is the only group of questions that were collected together. Placed at the end, in order to avoid giving any misleading impressions, they proved more productive than had been anticipated, partly because by then the interviewees had enjoyed the experience and gained complete confidence. They were asked, Is there anything you would be prepared to use the word 'sacred' of?; Whether or not you yourself would use the word 'holy', what would it mean to you?; and, What would you mean if you described somebody as 'truly religious'?

The interviews 'worked' extremely well. On the one hand, only one person ever declined to answer one question! Yet even he provided perfectly useful and useable material, completing the process in forty minutes. Everyone else enjoyed the experience ('No one ever asked me what I thought, before'), and took an hour or two. Several took four hours - and then said, 'You know, you should come back in six months (or, a year), and see what I say then'.

The 'pilot' interviews emboldened me to add in the questions on fear and dying, embarrassment and (at the very end) identity. Yet the sheer efficacy of the *stimuli* (as they may accurately be called) in 'lubricating' the responses (with that single exception), was surprising. Indeed, as the interviewees were told at the start that the purpose was to discover what they already felt and thought, and not to think up answers to questions on which they had no views, they had in fact been positively encouraged to decline to answer anything they so wished.

A decade or two later, first Robert Towler's investigation of *Common and Conventional Religion in Leeds*, and then the *European Value System Studies*, showed that 'qualitative' research can be conducted with large numbers, making scientific randomisation possible, and yet using pre-coded answers, making statistical analysis feasible. However, such resources were unavailable for open-ended qualitative investigations in 1968-9. So the hundred interviewees were simply selected according to their estimated willingness to speak their mind, and keeping a reasonable balance regarding gender, educational attainment, and degree of explicit-religious involvement. Seven of those asked, declined to be interviewed.

The Analysis
The presentation of the results was marked by serendipity. Thirty-six of the interviews had their response to each stimulus in turn compared. This revealed that the majority held the same opinion, while most of the rest held a second view, and some view predominated among the remainder. A 'spokesperson' was therefore selected from each of the three groups, so as to typify the whole spectrum of opinion. The three comprised something like an 'identi-kit' picture: a cross-section of the whole.

The three responses to each of the stimuli were then reflected upon, for anything up to an hour for each of them. What did they say, and assume? What did they deny or ignore? The process was, perhaps, comparable to that in which a literary critic ponders the meaning of a poem - or a disciple meditates on the implications of his Master's saying. It used the recorded words to try and enter into the mind of the speaker as completely as possible - and then looked at what it found there, from as many different viewpoints as possible. It strove to 'read out of' the text, while trying not to 'read into' it, other than self-consciously and comparatively.

Forty Themes seemed to emerge from the resulting commentary on the text. They were first grouped into fours, and then the ten quartets were themselves grouped, under the headings of The Inner Scene, The Outer Scene and The Other Scene. In other words, as with the invention of the questions and composition of the schedule, and as with the selection of the data and composition of the threefold identi-kit pictures, so with their analyses and conclusions: the intention was to discover any individual stones that were available, and only build them into a single wall as far as they would comfortably allow.

The interview questions themselves have since been borrowed and/or developed by a number of other students. They, and the fifty trios of responses, are reproduced here as an Invitation to reflection and analysis. A fuller report upon the interviewer's own analysis can be found in my *Implicit Religion in Contemporary Society*. Kok Pharos,1997: 77-128), where the forty Themes are likewise 'de-coded'. In this context, the findings may simply be illustrated and summarised.

The commitments

The outstanding impression left by the analysis, was of the position held by the Self. The use of the initial capital letter, which might be considered somewhat American, or Hindu, conveys, quickly and obviously, the flavour of this fundamental apprehension.

The impression that was gained and given, was of individuals being basically convinced that they were themselves of supreme value; but it wasn't quite as simple as that might suggest. It was rather that they 'had' a Self, and that that was of supreme value. They themselves, to a considerable extent, both watched, and watched over, this Self. They observed *its* ups-and-downs, and took care of it. They noticed how both they and it were continually changing, with the passage of time (hence the invitation to re-interview, later). They observed it come to life in relationships. They held it in some awe. It was the most sacred phenomenon in their experience. But it was simply - their selves. To have made it into an other, or spoken of it as an Other, would have seemed mystical and high-falutin', schizophrenic and self-righteous. They were, after all, 'only human'. But, they couldn't deny, they did have gifts, and the chief one was to have, or be, a Self.

Many of the other Themes seemed to be expressions of this core intuition. Ethics, for instance, was based upon the supposition that, if it would hurt me, it will hurt them, for we each have a similar Self. A question about dying voluntarily showed that respondents had already thought a lot about the subject: they *hoped* they would risk their own life to save someone else's, and thought they might even die *for* a person, but they were clear that they would not die for any kind of 'general cause'. Epistemology, so far as understanding other people is concerned (and that is the most important part), works on the same principle: if this is how I am, and function, so must they be.

From the point of view of social studies, it was interesting to see how content people were with their usual 'Round'. They were 'happy' to be burdened with a 'list' of 'jobs to be done'; they shouldered a burden of sympathy with those who suffer; they were unable to imagine what they would do with a 'really large win on the Pools'; they were 'very pleased' with any day that was filled with good relationships and jobs done. There was little sign of alienation, but much emphasis upon an alternative Round (rather than an alternative Reality). It consisted of *finishing* working (for others) each day, of going away on holiday each year, and of keeping family festivals, such as Christmas.

From the point of view of religious studies (or of philosophical theology), it was interesting to notice that the Self seemed to be *valued*, first, and only as a consequence of that was its existence posited. Of course it is difficult to make such conceptual or temporal distinctions, in such infinitesimal (or infinite), 'nuclear' moments, which have such intense power, to give both heat and light. But certainly the sequence seemed different from that often anticipated (eg that God, or any phenomenon, first *is*, and only then *does*). Yet it seems true to the greater features of life, such as falling in love. Psychologically, if not logically, the external first impinges on us as valuable, and only then becomes real.

From the point of view of the Christian religion, it is interesting to note the contrast between this emphasis upon the Self, as valuable and, in effect, as a locus of sacredness, which was as ultimate as it is intimate, on the one hand, and, on the other, Christianity, at least as taught by the Churches. A modern view of the twofold Commandment, To love God and to love one's neighbour as oneself, may expound it as basically threefold, on the grounds that loving oneself is a necessary part of the dynamic of the other two parts (as cause and/or as consequence). But this impression has been neither given nor gained, in the past or now. Certainly, hymns have spoken of the *soul*; but even were that to be identified with the Self, it is usually in connection with extra blessings bestowed, or duties urged, upon the soul, not the soul as simply one's own existence.

The second predominant string in the bow of the implicit religion revealed by the interviews, was the value placed upon the human. The Self was the ultimate location of the sacred, as has been said; and that was only saved from becoming an insufferable

49

pietistic egotism, by the insistence that I (like everyone else) am 'only human'. The adjective (*human*) was virtually never used without the dismissive qualifier (*only*). But occasionally someone like Winston Churchill was described in terms that began to clarify the width of the total spectrum covered by that adjective. For he was simultaneously 'gloriously' human, as well as 'only human' - and, it was felt, he couldn't have been so gloriously human, had he not been, and recognised that he was, '*only* human'. (Eisenhower, it was said, hardly passed that second test.)

The Self is revealed in the interviews, then, less as a theophany, than as a hierophany; or, to be more precise, as an 'anthropophany'. It, and human-ity, respectively, are the sacred, and the ideal.

6   IMPLICIT RELIGION: IN A PUBLIC HOUSE

The interviews with individuals gave opportunity for the description of peak experiences; but they were also, and more importantly, occasions for describing long-term commitments of various kinds (positive and negative, ideal and actual, conceptual and emotional). The introduction to the interviews had emphasised that whatever the interviewees themselves felt about any question, was exactly the 'right' answer, and the interviewer had taken care to avoid suggesting any other sort of criterion during the process, for instance by devotedly noting down every word that was said. Nevertheless, they were with individuals, and the stimulus for the response had come from the interviewer.

A second string to the bow of empirical observation (to test the practical viability and utility of the concept of implicit religion) was therefore tried. To work behind the bar of a pub, it seemed, would give an opportunity to view an important element within contemporary society, which was independent of church religion, and in a context where the observer could hardly have influenced the actual data, in their raw state, even if he had so wished. A student, seeking work, therefore, he spent a hundred four-hour sessions, consisting of week-end lunch-times or any evening, during the course of nine months, and also visited the same pub as a customer over the course of a couple of years.

The public house
The pub was built in 1939, a mile from the centre of Bristol, by the side of a busy main road. Its customers, like myself, came on foot, from the nineteenth-century 'suburbs' surrounding it. Our general tenor was urban, traditional, and respectable. The public (bar) side was almost a 'study in brown', with something of the austerity of an old schoolroom or Territorial Army drill-hall, epitomised by the linoleum on the floor. The lounge side was a warmer red, reminiscent of a petty-bourgeois sitting-room, with a carpet on the floor. Each side had a living fire, and a recently installed 'fruit-box' or 'machine'. (By 1980 each side had been converted into a 'Victorian snug', but with extra 'machines' in place of the fires.)

The observation

Bars are sometimes pictured as some kind of confessional. No doubt the life of each pub is different, as with churches, parishes, or schools. However, there was little scope in the dynamics of this pub for such 'confessions'. The early evening was too quiet for a truly private conversation; the later evening was too busy for the barmen to linger. Certainly, the personal talk that did occur, was encouraged more by the accepting environment (or the anonymity of a casual visit), than by the effects of the alcohol. Yet such conversations were limited, both in number and extent, compared to those experienced in many other contexts, such as the professions, or between female friends, or indeed in the interviews. Observation centred, therefore, as intended, upon the life of the whole clientèle, as illustrated and commented upon by individuals, rather than upon their own life-histories.

Following each session, the all-important 'diary' was compiled, recording conversations and observations, and beginning the process of ordering and analysis.

The integrating foci

Seven 'integrating foci' were discovered in the life of the pub. First was the idea of the English/British pub, which is cultivated by the advertisers and reflected back by foreigners. It is expressed verbally in the belief that 'you get all types in a pub'. This catholicity may be limited, in comparison with a doctor's waiting-room or a church, but it represents a real transcendence of social divisions, in a setting that is primarily social. It also represents a degree of pride in such a basic human equality.

To a lesser degree, its being the 'local' of those that do come, it also becomes a 'local' for those in the vicinity that do not. For them, of course, the fact, of the building's presence and purpose, is more prominent, than the character of the social life within it. But, as is well-known, regardless of use, every community likes to know that it has at least one pub (and post office, school, church and open space).

The pub as an idea, and the pub as a building, form two, inter-dependent, foci. Another such pair, are the doorway between

52

the two sides, and the sides themselves. They, however, are so closely bound together, as to form a single focus.

A division between the two sides was legally and commercially necessary, for it designated the area in which 'bitter' (beer) was sold at the statutorily decreed price. The doorway between the two sides was equally necessary, on practical grounds, because it enabled the single set of staff to divide their attention between the two sides. It also enabled those items that were kept on the public (bar) side, such as cigarettes, to be brought through to the lounge side; and those items that were kept on the lounge side, such as cigars, to be carried through to the public bar. However, the doorway, like the two sides, functioned in the realm of meaning, as well as practicality.

The existence of two sides reflects in principle the class structure that is to be found in British society, as elsewhere. In the world of the pub, however, the customer can choose for himself with which class (in this mythopeoically simplified structure) he will identify. He can in fact 'class-ify' himself. So each 'side' needs the other, to complete their world. But for it to be a single world, with an overarching/underlying unity, it is also necessary for there to be a doorway. The pub's 'doorway', lacking both door or even curtain, fulfilled the purpose admirably; for customers on each side could spy out the lie of the land on the other, which they regularly did. Indeed, those on the lounge side sometimes commented that it 'must be nicer' serving on their side; while those in the bar complained that they were being neglected.

This symbolic significance manifested itself in the hostility to the suspected desire of the breweries to do away with the public side in the pubs that they owned. They were accused of wanting to increase the price of the bitter, to match that in the lounge. However, it seemed that the loss of 'principle', of some sort, counted for more than a small increase in price. The principle could hardly claim any longer to be the duty of hospitality to travellers. It seemed more likely that it was the 'democratic' (or corporatist, or 'totalist') principle: that 'you [can] get all types in a pub'.

Perhaps the difference can be sensed (as an omission, merely) upon entering an American pub. 'My greenback is as good as his', in each case. The décor, and even the local roots, are not altogether different. But in the American parallel, the customer does not have the freedom to categorise himself in a way that is specific to the situation. To do so, requires both distinction, and mutual recognition: two sides, with a 'door' way in between them. The alternative is either a cafe, or else two separate clubs.

The first and second of the integrating foci (the myth and the physical structure) were distinct and yet inter-dependent. Thus they were like the third, the two sides that were joined together phenomenally and phenomenologically by their inter-communicating doorway. The fourth focus is also a duality (the bar on each of the sides), but in this case each of them, in parallel, independently integrates the life of its own side.

The bar on the public side runs down almost the whole length of the room, emphasising its narrow rectangularity. The bar in the lounge is semi-circular, because the 'second half' of that side of the building is occupied by the Ladies' (accessed from this 'side') and the Gents' (accessed from the other 'side').

Each of the bars is a spectacular piece of woodwork; and each is carefully maintained. Cigarettes may have been surreptitiously stubbed out against the painted support on the public side, but the visible and beautiful bar proper will be 'wiped down' by the customers themselves, if the 'bar-men' haven't time to do so. For it has come to mean, less a 'bar-rier' (to public access to the private living quarters), than a table top. It could hardly be treated with greater respect, if it had been decreed to be sacred.

The fifth focus is the 'busy time'. This starts at 9.0, or 9.30, and lasts until Closing Time, at 10.30 (in 1970). It is a distinct part of the evening. A couple of couples in the lounge may prefer to go, before 'it gets too busy' (noisy, crowded). Yet (even for them, probably), it is the climax of the evening: it's what everyone's been waiting for, and when the pub comes to life.

Lunch-times, for instance, have a different feel about them. This is partly because they lack the finality of night-time closing. Yet it is mainly because they lack this climactic conclusion, with its *drawing* power, upon the whole of the rest of the opening-time.

The sixth focus is the Manager. With him are coupled the barmen (there was only one girl in nine months, out of a dozen assorted assistants), for they are extensions of his *persona*, and chosen by him. He presides over the whole, and (ideally) incarnates its spirit. It is his *role* to be himself, i.e. to be personal. So he greets and serves every regular upon their arrival, or, if that is not possible because he is already serving (on the other side), then, when he sees them, he calls across to them at the table where they are sitting.

He is also the butt for various complaints, during those quiet hours before the 'busy time'. The regulars say they've 'never known it so quiet'. They find a different reason every month ('saving up for Christmas', 'getting over Christmas', 'too cold to go out', 'too hot to stay in'); but ultimately it's the Manager's fault. It's all because, 'He's only a manager, not a landlord, [you] see'; so he 'doesn't care', it 'stands to reason'; 'you can tell [that] by the way he gives you your change: slams it down [on the bar], like that [with the fingers over the coins]'.

The last of the seven integrating foci is the 'transaction' of 'giving' the drink and 'giving' the money. It is described in that way because to call it 'buying' and 'selling' would smack of statistics, rather than the lived data. It might represent the economics, but it would not describe the experience. What is being 'purchased' is something spiritual (in both senses, usually). It is not simply the legitimating charter of the pub, of the barman's work, and of the customer's presence; it is also a 'welcome', epitomised in 'mine host'.

This focus has been placed last, because it is probably the most important of all, at a personal level, and in ways that are not always recognised (at least by less regular users). It may help to explain the ubiquity of the saying about 'going to a pub for a drink', when it is quite clear that that is not why people come to the pub. As one regular, at the public bar, said (more than once): 'I don't know why I come, really. I always keep a couple of bottles of every thing - gin, whiskey, sherry, the lot - in the house; but I never drink at home, when I'm alone' - meaning, with his wife, but without any other 'company'. Only once, in four hundred hours, was a customer observed to come in, apparently, because he was thirsty, and so just 'for a drink'. Similarly, every single customer whose habits could be observed, over however many nights and purchases, always had the very same drink, or else alternated between the same pair of drinks, regardless of the weather, their palate - or the choice available.

The first stage in the ritual of the transaction was the 'entrance'. This, it has to be said, was somewhat nerve-wracking, even for the most faithful of the regulars. It may, indeed, be one reason why many people do not go to pubs - and one reason why the Manager tries to greet every arrival, old and new, personally. The next stage is the 'placing of the order', involving the right terminology on the one side, and the provision of the right kind of glass ('sleever' or 'handle', for instance), on the other. Then there is the proffering, not of the right coinage, but, at least in this pub at that time, of the largest note available. For the dynamic of the pub is not that of rational economics, but of (an officially) 'licensed' *potlach*. Then there is the giving of the change. This was not counted; for the economics is that of a 'divine' anti-economy. These mutual and 'personal' parts were often accompanied by funny stories or other conversation.

Finally (for this was often the sequence), if the 'customer' was one of a group, he then recalled their requests, and placed their orders, and proffered payment (usually, without knowing how much was needed, or taken.

Thus the entrance and its consummation had something of the feel of a dramatic, group initiation (albeit repeated nightly), and a slower more personal communion, between the initiand and the institution's representative.

These seven foci may provide, in miniature, a picture which is recognisable to those familiar with the life of pubs, and imagine-able to any who are not. The full report discusses the place of 'Christianity' within the pub, the parallels between this local pub and the 'typical' local Church, and asks whether they are seen as rivals, or as complementary crucibles of celebratory spirituality. Here, though, the question must simply be, What sort of religiosity, if any, is implicit within its life, and to what extent, or in what way, is it religious?

The inner meaning, it is suggested, and the dominant power, within the pub, is the strength of its community feeling. This is never mentioned, except negatively: in complaints about the

Manager, whose unitive function is therefore that of both presiding bishop and proverbial scapegoat.

It is, nevertheless, daily demonstrated, above all at closing time. Then the regulars, not least (but not only) the male darts players (some of whom are unmarried) will seemingly continue to find one reason after another to delay their departure, like children testing the strength of their membership, trying the sense of community, stretching the covenant relationship, confirming its reality. It was also, however, demonstrated by the extreme 'moral' pressure with which the regulars were able to insist upon each other's presence 'this evening', or to enquire after 'backsliding'. The light-hearted veneer was hardly even intended to cover a seriousness which few ministers of religion would dare adopt with their flock.

'Community', however, is a less appropriate description than something like 'solidarity'. For the pub is less a community than a 'scene', in which an archipelago, of small groups at the tables, and of individuals at the bars, compose themselves into a communality. Were this to be expressed in terms of a single idea, ideal, or myth, then it could be described as providing the context in which to 'be a man'.

By 'being a man' is primarily meant, not the contrast with younger age-groups, although they are prohibited from entering; nor with the opposite sex, although they seldom came without male company; nor with any natural, or supernatural, referent. It meant, above all, proving the ability to 'hold your own', as one regular put it, when describing (in effect) 'how to succeed in a strange pub without [and this was the essential point] apparently really trying'. The phrase may originate in some kind of person-to-person combat (cudgelling, duelling, fisticuffs); now it means 'holding your liquor' (which is taken for granted) and, more significantly, 'holding your own with [N.B.] others'.

This diagnosis was clearly and quietly confirmed on the one occasion that a customer was asked to leave (i.e. temporarily excommunicated) 'until he could behave'. A visitor from another part of the country, he had had a little too much to drink (as indicated, for instance, by his unsought criticisms of this particular city). He also bought a drink, for everyone else he could. He thus doubly demonstrated his inability to be both independent and equal: to be himself (his own self), and simultaneously let others be themselves (their selves). He hadn't learned how to be a man.

A threefold division is common within the study of the (recognised) religions. Indeed, it reflects human life generally. So the implicit religion of the pub may likewise be described as possessing three facets. They are the ritual activity of 'having a drink', the communal solidarity of the initiates, and the mental (mythical and ethical) rationale of 'being a man'.

1. 'Having a drink'. *Ritual Activity*

2. Community solidarity & initiates

3. Being a man.

7 IMPLICIT RELIGION: IN A SUBURB

In searching for what might be described as the implicit religion of contemporary society, the interviews revealed some of the 'human depths' (the fourth possible definition of what is sought) of some typical individuals. The public house, on the other hand, had shown individuals operating together in a public situation that was more clearly unaffected by the observer. However, it seemed desirable to look for 'implicit religion' in a more 'natural' situation than either the interviews or the pub. A community, of some seven thousand people, on the outskirts of the city, would have the advantage of including all ages, and largely excluding any element of self-selection. There is also something stable about any study based on three legs: conclusions resting on a tripod appealed, as seeming more secure.

However, this was not all thought up *ab initio*. On the contrary, it was after offering to help out with the odd duty in a parish, and being asked to look after this one during its interregnum, that the possibility occurred. Then, following the Churchwardens' suggestion, and finding a certain affinity with the parish, the planned two or three months of (what anthropologists call) participant observation, became twenty-eight years (to date) of what may perhaps better be called, 'observant participation'.

The participation
In 1970 the role of the Rector of a parish would have appeared a dubious standpoint from which to make observations that were neither skewed by the character of the available data nor biassed by theological interpretation. The social and cultural and intellectual reasons for the change in that attitude, between (say) the 1960s and the 1980s, typify those wider developments, that were mentioned in the first chapter. On the one hand, experience showed (and reflection suggested, to those without such experience) that people were not so lacking in *amour-propre* (or so dependent upon the Rector's opinion) as unduly to tailor their behaviour in his presence; nor would he (or their peers) necessarily be incapable of detecting such a modification (which would no more earn his approval than theirs).

On the other hand, his position not only gave him some degree of access to virtually any member of the community, but his role, as perceived by the community, gives him access to a very wide range of human life. A single morning may include practical questions about pensions, poltergeists, and attitudes to divorce and re-marriage among Moslems in East Africa, for instance. The afternoon may include discussion of their deepest beliefs and experiences, with parents who want their baby Baptised; discussing their departed, while with a newly bereaved family; and discussing the possibility of re-marriage in church, with a couple, one of whom has been divorced. The evening might include a consideration of the nature of Christian and human life, with Confirmation candidates who are aged thirteen or in their middle age or old age - followed by a meeting of the Church Council to do with the accounts, with buildings, and with evangelism, or a meeting of the School Governors to do with the curriculum and staff appointments.

It is growing awareness of such realities, and appreciation of our ignorance of them, that lie behind such slogans (or newly coined proverbs) as, 'Small is beautiful', 'If it isn't local, it isn't real', 'Think globally, act locally'; and behind such abstract principles as 'pluralism', or 'subsidiarity', or even, 'privatisation'. Obsolete metaphors such as 'market' forces, using ill-considered myths, can still mislead, so that 'parochial' continues to mean 'narrow'. Yet 'the parish pump' can now again be seen, not only as a source of an essential amenity, but also as an occasion for social interaction (as context for the *water of life*, physical and spiritual).

The diary of record that was kept of the pub, in the parish became a diary of engagements (over a thousand planned ones a year), a minority of which were, at best, followed by Minutes. Detailed recording was out of the question, especially of an interaction that was almost as continuous as that of an unemployed family all living at home. Recording and reflection has, therefore, tended to take place approximately annually, often during a holiday- (or retreat-)-like week or two in the summer. However, less systematically, and therefore often either merged or forgotten, observation and analysis has, of course, gone on daily, even hourly; so that it has become 'second(?) nature'.

To report upon a relatively holistic universe requires selection. Even full-length 'community studies' necessitate omission, and concentrate, in order to clarify. 'Implicit religion' (like 'religion', if not more so) is interested in the whole of life; but, like religion, being human and finite, is concerned with the whole, from a particular position. This viewpoint is situated within culture and consciousness.

That is not to say, that it is not concerned with the practical as well as the symbolic (with agri-culture, for instance, as with human culture). Most symbols, including the most powerful, are, indeed, at least in part, natural, rather than artificial: more akin to the sun or the human body, than to the Church's crossed keys or industry's logo's. It is to say, though, that in a world where such inter-woven dimensions of human existence have been distinguished, the particular and peculiar contribution to the whole that the study of religion, and implicit religion, can offer, is mental more than material. In effect, however, that will mainly mean the mental aspects of the material dimensions (the word *for* bread).

The overall life of this community, therefore, is sketched in terms of the character of its general consciousness.

The community
There is an ambiguity regarding the referent of its name: 'Winterbourne' can still refer to the settlement around the five-armed cross-roads at one end of the half-mile High Street, leaving 'Watley's End' to describe the later, eighteenth century settlement that is a further half mile from the other end of the High Street. Alternatively, especially with the in-filling of the space between them, Winterbourne can now refer, existentially as well as by statute, to both 'ends', as parts of a single community.

Yet again, Winterbourne can still refer to that whole (the ecclesiastical parish), plus the two adjacent ecclesiastical parishes of Winterbourn [*sic*] Down and Frenchay; for the continuing civil parish has never been divided. But that meaning is largely restricted, formally and existentially, to the Parish Councillors themselves.

Rolls-Royce and British Aerospace, three or four miles away at Filton and Patchway, used to be the largest single

61

employers. However, the main sources of employment, situated within the community itself, are its disproportionate number of schools. For many of those who live in the parish either work in them, or at other schools nearby. Many other members of the community have somewhat similar careers: in the social services, or as draughtsmen or computer programmers, or commercial representatives using the nearby rail and motorway intersections. So parishioners as a whole not only have the usual keen interest in their children's and grandchildren's schooling, but also sustain an impressive number and range of out-of-school activities, both for children and adults.

It is therefore possible, following the pattern of Bede's '*Ecclesiastical* History of England', to regard the parish as an '*educational* community'. Indeed, as its geographical character was illustrated by the various meanings of its official name, so its demographic development is indicated by the story of its schools.

The first school, in what was then the undivided, civil-cum-ecclesiastical, parish, was founded by a committee of Churchpeople from Bristol (eight miles away), which included William Wilberforce, the MP who was a leading campaigner against the slave trade. They met in 1813 at the pub which stands at the junction of the roads from Bristol and the subsequent Winterbourn Down, where a room was also temporarily made available for the school. By 1815 the new school was ready, at the point where the road from Frenchay, with its large houses, just outside the city boundary (and the restrictions of the 1662 Five mile Act), joined with the road from Winterbourn Down, just inside the boundary of the (ecclesiastical) parish.

In 1868, however, the school was moved to a point midway along the High Street, opposite the Rectory. Each position in turn exactly suited the intended catchment area of the day, for, first Frenchay, in 1834, and then Winterbourn Down, in 1858, had become separate ecclesiastical parishes, with their own Church schools.

The changing plan of the school was similarly too precise to be accidental, for in 1815 the school had basically met in the schoolmaster's (large, purpose-built) house. However, in 1868 the schoolmaster's house was built cheek-by-jowl with the school (with shared plumbing, until 1979), exactly as much distinct as it was adjacent.

The next school to arrive in the parish (in 1945, from Bristol) was a small, independent, all-age, day and boarding school for girls. It gradually established increasing contact with the locality, in terms of pupils, staff, and services, but had to close in 1991. The following year the site was taken over by another independent school, but, with an existing staff and no boarders, there was little formal local contact.

The next school within the 'maintained' system, therefore, was the secondary modern, catering not only for Winterbourne, but also for Winterbourn Down on the Bristol side, and Frampton Cotterell and Coalpit Heath (and Iron Acton, beyond) in the Yate direction. Built on the High Street, which marks the edge of Winterbourne's housing, its playing field a mile away, it likewise could hardly have had a more central site for its catchment area. Its head, who for twenty years oversaw its continual stop-go expansion, and its conversion to comprehensive status in the 1960s, and the postponement of the school-leaving age to sixteen in the 1970s, bought his own house, yet within the parish - and, indeed, retired to it.

With the growth in the population of the (ecclesiastical) parish in the 1960s, from about 2,000 people to about 7,000, a new Primary School was built in 1961, closer to Watley's End (under County auspices this time). This and the Church of England (Voluntary, Controlled - that is, controlled by the County) School were subsequently divided into Junior and Infant Schools (in 1966 and 1970, respectively). So in the 1970s the parish had five schools, in addition to the independent one.

In 1979 the two parallel pairs were each re-amalgamated, into two Primaries. Pupils at the secondary school likewise fell, from virtually 2,000 to 1,200, in the 1980s. In the 1990s all three remaining local schools have climbed again, following the widening of their potential catchment areas. During this decade, many of those who first bought their semi-detached house in the 1960s, whose children have been through these schools, have retired, and are themselves entering their sixties.

63

This 'educational' parish has a considerable sense of identity. The judgement is based in the first place upon their saying that 'Winterbourne is a nice place to live', or that, 'People say it's nice'. Their sincerity is borne out by the general (but not overwhelming) desire to continue living here; so that many who moved in, shortly after marrying in the sixties, are still living in the same house, with the same neighbours. The reality of this sense of identity tends to be confirmed, rather than questioned, by their low-key approach to it.

This judgement appearing apt, it is possible to see reasons for the sense of identity. In the first place, the community in the built-up part of the parish is fairly clearly bounded: by fields on two sides, and, on the other two, by the railway line that marks the junction with Winterbourn Down, and by the road that marks the boundary with Frampton Cotterell. Thus the community is visible as a single unit, sitting up on its slightly elevated plateau. The neighbouring parishes are (with a single exception) all smaller, but they tend to project the same, village-like image, back upon this one.

A second cluster of reasons, however, arises from the way in which the village grew, in the 1960s. For it was, above all, piecemeal. This means that the Council's houses were not all built at one end; that many roads include both types of housing; that the larger roads have houses of different design, often built at different times, by different firms; and, last but not least, that many of them are in one of what are (in effect) twenty-nine different cul-de-sacs or 'closes'.

This sense of identity has been tested and proved by the intermittent challenges to it during these twenty-eight years. The loss of a number of old and/or odd internal landmarks has been regretted, but accepted with the usual resigned comment, 'Well, that's progress, I suppose'. The unusual combination of gemeinschaft and gesellschaft (sensed in 1970) has, however, evoked national comment on the reactions when the community's distinct identity has been threatened; in particular, by the Severnside Study in 1973, by the Avon County plan in 1979, by a repeated application to build a further 2,000 houses in the Frome Valley in the 1980s, and by British Aerospace's proposal to commercialise its runways at Patchway in the mid-1990s.

The character of this relaxed but vigilant sense of identity is similarly pluralistic, yet cohesive. The parish is not uniform, but the differences are acknowledged. For instance, probably by a mixture of good management and good luck, the usual contrasts (economic, social, cultural, denominational, and length of residence), which might have coincided geographically and then become polarised, in fact became increasingly muddled as development proceeded, and thus became less dichotomous. We may not advertise our idiosyncratic views, and we may lack the confidence to enter into dialogue, but it is seldom necessary to pretend positive agreement, when certainty is in fact lacking.

No two parishes are ever alike - any more than schools, pubs, people, or fingerprints. However, this one was shrewdly described in the late 1970s, by a 'parish worker' with considerable experience in this country and abroad, as being 'unusually normal'.

Intensive concerns, with extensive effects

If this is the character of its general consciousness (sitting upon the rest of its existence, as the tip of an ice-berg rests upon its floating foundation), what, then, are the integrating foci within that consciousness? Six intensive concerns, that have extensive effects, have been identified.

First, children have been described as its wilful divinities. However, if 'divinities' is taken in too God-like a manner, then perhaps 'sprites' (like the spirits associated with trees, by those living in a jungle) might convey the intention more accurately.

Bodies, especially, are 'hedged about with divinity', because, emerging out of the systems of the universe, they yet have personality. By this is meant that they have character, will, and the ability to bestow a blessing (or to give cause for concern). The young baby is the type-case. When it smiles, 'all's right with the world'. However, the type-case has value in understanding reactions to all ages. Further reflection (now while writing this, in fact) suggests that this is a parallel, within the parish, to the primary conclusion from the Interviews: that the Self is sacred, both in spite of, and because of, its being human.

Not unrelated to that focus (it now seems) is a second. Friendly, is its revelatory ethic. By this is meant that when someone (especially someone who is in some kind of authority, and/or someone whom we cannot help dealing with, such as a neighbour), is friendly towards us, we respond, as to sunshine: God's in his heaven, and the world is a good place. The symbol of this imperative is the smile; and, while that may not be as demanding or dramatic as a cross, it may nevertheless demonstrate goodwill, and require a certain sacrificial effort.

The third may seem paradoxical. The parish's profoundest solidarity is expressed in, and may be expressed as a result of, its very individualism. Generally, this takes the form of an attitude which could be articulated as: In so much of my life, I have to do this and do that, at certain times in specific places under particular conditions, that I insist on doing my own thing, for some of my time. This will often take the form of doing nothing; thereby proving, above all to myself, that I *am* my own person, after all. Occasionally, it will take a shared form (spoken or unspoken): 'No one's going to push me around - and don't you let them tell you what to do, either'.

Fourthly, buildings are the community's sacramental language. That they have a symbolic significance has long been widely appreciated, within the community. The Scout leaders, like the Community Association, said (in 1973, and 1971, respectively) that that was a chief, and a sufficient, reason, for their wanting a home of their (corporate) own. That they are of (implicit-) religious significance, can hardly be doubted, in view of the sacrifices of time, energy and money devoted to the family home, and, in some cases, to such corporate homes. Indeed, they fulfil a similar function, in this domesticated culture, to that occupied by land in an agrarian society, or animals in a pastoral or hunting economy. (That this was predictable, on theoretical grounds, only dawned, following the empirical observation.)

This explains the fifth focus which has been identified, against all expectations. The church (building) is the major symbol of the community. Here, as in so many settlements worldwide, the religious building was virtually the first major one to be built. It is still the only truly public one. It remains therefore the community's main 'distinguishing' mark (as the application forms for passports say). Of (hidden) use to many who hardly ever use it visibly, it can be compared with those who are said to 'serve, but only stand and wait'.

The depth of this reality, was vividly demonstrated in 1989 at a public meeting regarding the route of a new by-pass. The planners confessed they were not surprised by the universal condemnation of routing it between the High Street and the church (leaving the church, not only out in the fields, but cut off from the houses); but, they said, they had to suggest that possibility, for the very reason that it was the most obvious route.

Finally, again against the grain of my own expectations, 'Christianity' is its professed faith. The first response to such a deep confession as, 'Well, you see, I believe in Christianity', must be to ask what is meant by 'Christianity' (and by 'believe'). But it is certainly 'confessed', as an ideal, of which one is unworthy: as a transcendental experience is confessed; as a truth about one's self is confessed; as sin is confessed. Whatever one is to make of them, they are facts. Only secondly may one usefully or legitimately begin to compare such a finding with any other understanding of the terms involved, such as their canonical definition.

'Christianity', in this context, seems to have three sides: belief in God, in Christ, and in the church. But none of those is itself central; in the way that belief in the LORD, or faith in Christ, is often seen as central in the two Testaments. They are aspects of 'Christianity', but not themselves the object of the belief. That object of belief would appear to be a spirit. It is characterised by love.

That, of course, is reported in this context as an empirical statement. The conclusions may be drawn from it, for religion or society, fall outside the scope of this volume.

ITS IMPORTANCE

Placing implicit religion within
its context

(1) relationship ō explicit religion
(2) spiritual education
(3) current pointes towards future
developments

8 EXPLICIT RELIGION AND IMPLICIT RELIGION

The concept of 'implicit religion' was defined in terms of three possible synonyms: 'commitments', or 'integrating foci', or 'intensive concerns with extensive effects'. But the reality to which the concept refers was also described with the help of various negative cautions, in the hope of avoiding possible misunderstandings. For instance, it was said that the use of the term 'religion' was not seen either as a compliment or its opposite. It was also said that, while any particular form of implicit religion might be related to a particular form of explicit religion in all sorts of ways (as its historical origin or legacy, as its social basis or enemy, as its phenomenological source or goal, as its spiritual mentor or disciple, as its inspiration or by-product), there was no assumption that implicit religion in general bore any relationship whatsoever with any form of explicit religion. It was also insisted that the formulation of the concept was aimed at assisting in the understanding of people, not at asserting the universality among human beings of some attribute that can be labelled 'religious'.

Thirty years later, the use of the concept retains all three forms of self-limitation. It is a heuristic hypothesis, which avoids any assumptions of an evaluative, comparative, or anthropological nature. Restricting attention, in this way, to its meaning and core purpose has helped to demonstrate its power to enlighten, without being side-tracked by the heat that such issues can engender. What others might make of any findings, for their own ideological or practical purposes, was not considered pertinent to this central focus, on the *study* of implicit religion.

In the context of this general Introduction, however, some consideration of the wider ramifications, of both the concept and its application, is in order. Thus the very use of the noun 'religion', raises questions regarding the relationship of 'explicit religion' to implicit religion. Likewise, the re-discovery of the concept of 'spirituality' (and the practical concern with 'spiritual education'), during the 1980s, arouses interest in the relationship between the spiritual and the implicit-religious. Lastly, the co-incidence of the 'post-modern' hypothesis with the start of a new millennium, increases interest in the possible future relevance of the concept, in both religious and secular settings. As the first four chapters, then, were largely 'experiential' (or existential), and then gave way to a trio of empirical applications of the hypothesis, so these three concluding chapters will move into a more exploratory or speculative mode. (Their overall theme is set out diagrammatically in the first of the appended 'Invitations'.)

'Implicit' or 'explicit' religion the analogy?
So far as the relationship between implicit and explicit religion is concerned, a cluster of questions can be summed up by assessing the status of the noun, 'religion', in the very suggestion that an 'implicit' form of religion is possible.

On the one hand, for instance, are (or were, in the 1960s and '70s) standing those scholarly and religious observers who wished to draw comparisons between commitments such as nationalism or secularism, baseball or football, children or nature, and what was conventionally called 'religion'. Referring to such secular look-alikes as 'quasi-religions' (or 'pseudo-religions'), the exact degree of recognition or cynicism given to them, depended partly upon the commentators' own estimates of the phenomena, and partly upon their estimate of their public's attitude to the comparison. On the other hand, standing opposite to this group, were some Christian clergy, who combined an early Barth with a Kierkegaardian Lutheranism, and equated all 'true' religion with an existentialist faith that could only be found *outside* the Churches. However, their Christocentrism effectively prevented their finding common cause with secular mysticism, public or private.

Consideration of the relation between explicit and implicit religion must begin by acknowledging that various phenomena that have been very diverse and widespread have, nevertheless, seemed to have some common characteristic and so have been given a common label. Their diversity of form has been so wide-ranging and profound, that the commonality would seem to lie in the realm of their (human) functioning. By a consent that is relatively common, this characteristic could be described as 'commitment'. However we may wish to describe this common core, some aspect of explicit religion has been sufficiently conspicuous to provide a

71

'type', which the concept of 'implicit religion' has been able to draw upon.

A second consideration is more speculative, and indeed provocative. Should it be agreed that some such human attribute as 'commitment' is, indeed, the *sine qua non* of what is meant by 'religion', then 'implicit religion' will refer to that which is the substance of all religion. So, instead of implicit religion being *analogous* to explicit religion (the 'real thing'), explicit religion will only actually be religious (as distinct from moral, political, social, cultural, aesthetic etc), when it is also in fact implicitly-religious.

As an estimate of the ontological reality of the phenomenon, rather than of its 'worth' within any wider frame of reference, this represents the contribution of the existentialist position.

Religion explicitly secondary
Are there any other grounds for advocating that the understanding of religion should focus upon its implicit rather than explicit forms?

The first such ground has already been indicated by the existentialist understanding - of what religion is, rather than of what it ought to be. Minus its *angst*, it is in fact the widespread, popular understanding of what the word itself does already mean (and, only consequently, of what religious practice should be like). It is perfectly demonstrated (in my hearing, weekly, if not daily), when people say, for instance: I read the [news] papers religiously. By it, they mean: regularly, but not compulsively; habitually, but not unthinkingly; deliberately, but not obsessively; voluntarily, but not arbitrarily; routinely, but by choice. Sometimes (in the Interviews, for instance) they make their meaning crystal clear, by conducting a mini-exercise in 'comparative religion'. They say (e.g.) 'She goes to church every Sunday, but her real religion is ... ' her family or money or whatever.

If the first ground for advocating this shift of focus in the understanding of religion is the popular usage of the term, then the second ground is religion's own understanding of itself.

On the one hand, the entire prophetic tradition (of which existentialist theology is a single, recent example) is based upon this insight into the nature of the phenomenon itself. For it is both broader and more basic (cp Otto and Durkheim) than the merely verbal, dialectical, and moral. The same characteristic is also present, on the other hand, within the sacramental tradition. For, whereas magic and superstition may concern the 'odd' and that which is disconnected with ordinary life, sacraments, by their very nature, unite the sacred with the secular, find meaning in the mundane, make the ordinary symbolic, elucidate the word that is within the bread, try turning water into wine.

If a third ground be allowed, it must be the apparent inadequacy of any understanding of religion that simply equates it with explicit religion. The popular mind may not be infallible, but neither is it to be despised. Religious virtuosi may only have partial experience, but they can be acute analysts (as well as profound critics) of what they do know. What cannot be supported, on empirical grounds, is that religion, in any form, *qua* religion, is ever only concerned with (explicit) religion. It is always, like magic, a means to an end; but religion's end may be the recognition of the autonomy of the inexplicable.

To 'pretend' (in either sense) that religion is a discrete function may be understandable, in view of the limited knowledge, say, of the *philosophes*. It may also be understandable, in view of prevailing conditions, say, in Northern Ireland. But such a claim is an ideological position or a political platform, not an empirical statement. It limited the religious, by its definition, to the superficial and so to the obsolescent. Strange to say, however, many of those who are most active in the 'religious' organisations have likewise tended to equate 'religion' with a single 'stage' in the development or spectrum of religiosity: that epitomised in the I-Thou encounter.

The practice of religion, and its study, then, need to take account of, on the one hand, both the explicitly religious, and its diametrical opposite, the explicitly anti-religious; and, on the other hand, that 'secular' area between these two ends of the spectrum, which can either be seen as implying explicit religion, or as implying a secular kind of religion (such as the politicians and advertisers try to discern). Beneath each of the two ends of the spectrum, and beneath both these central portions, lies an implicit religiosity.

This religiosity, and its expressions, will be integrated, only to the extent that intentionality, and thus identity itself, is integrated.

9 SPIRITUAL EDUCATION AND IMPLICIT RELIGION

Implicit religion differs from culture as a whole in being primarily concerned with the overall intentionality and consciousness revealed by human artefacts (of every kind, from words to deeds), and the response to them.   The history of religion as a whole suggests permanent underlying needs and archetypes.   At the same time, the history of particular religions demonstrates changes that are both rapid and profound.   So observation of implicit religion may likewise suggest underlying continuities, such as the recurrent return to the importance of the moral in English culture; and yet can pinpoint some significant changes to the year (or even more precisely).

One such change is the re-introduction of the concept of spirituality.   For the first half of the century the term was monopolised by explicit religion: typically, a Spiritual Director advised on habits of prayer, and offered the most appropriate moral guidance.   As a result, by a date two-thirds of the way through the century, the term was shunned, even by many of those who were most actively involved in organised religion.   Indeed, in 1966 itself I recall the term being introduced at a conference of high-minded, idealistic educationists and teachers, and being dismissed, with mixed incomprehension and disdain, especially by the men present.   Yet within twenty years, 'it was all the rage', in every walk of life - and an item for inspection in schools.   As religion was down-sized (and began to be distinguished from morality), so the necessity of the spiritual, in any understanding of the human, could be acknowledged.

It might seem as though Implicit Religion had indeed been given official recognition.   Perhaps the difference in terminology was only to prevent misunderstanding: 'implicit religion' might have suggested that the Government expected the pupils to develop an incipient Christianity (or Islam, etc).   That a somewhat different meaning was intended, was, however, suggested by the continuous listing of 'spiritual' *alongside* 'religious', suggesting (like the naming of 'moral' as well as 'emotional, 'social' as well as 'cultural') that, whatever the degree of their overlap, each was distinguishable from the other.

74

The purpose of this chapter is to explore the relationship of spirituality and implicit religion, by placing each of them in context, and both of them in a wider context. (The whole is set out, diagrammatically, in the first appended Invitation.)

'Spiritual' historically
One possible way to define the meaning of spirituality would be to describe its meaning for the cultural parents of contemporary culture. So, for instance, we might conclude that 'spiritual' in classical Greek thinking referred above all to that 'genius' of living individuality that inhabited every phenomenon, but reached its zenith in humans; while 'spiritual' in Judeo-Christian thought referred essentially to the relationships between phenomena, which could reach divine status in the relationship between persons. If the Hellenistic understanding points to that inner life that can be read from the light in the eyes, the Hebraic view points to that inner life that is expressed in the warmth of a greeting.

However, even if this kind of contrast is historically accurate, it no more describes what 'spirit', 'spiritual' and 'spirituality' mean in contemporary culture, than attempts to decide what *religio* meant in classical Latin can determine what 'religion' means today. Its classical progenitors (or, better, parallels) can suggest models for analysing the area (both of which we may consider useful), and phenomena for comparison. However, they cannot decide what it does mean, or should mean, now.

'Spiritual' today
What it should mean is not within the purpose of this volume. Regarding what it does mean, several points occur.

Firstly, the 'spiritual' is seen as referring to the non-physical. Secondly, the traditional (ecclesiastical) understanding of the 'spiritual' (as the disciplined development of that potential) causes no difficulty. Thirdly, the equally traditional understanding of the spiritual, as encompassing evil spirits (or neutral phenomena, such as ghosts), is readily understood.

Fourthly, the difference between the contemporary ('postmodern') meaning, and the traditional, premodern meaning,

75

lies in the relationship of the 'spiritual' and the 'physical' sides of existence. The warfare of a superior realm with an inferior realm, has been succeeded by the complementarity of a single pair of dimensions that together make up the whole. In Christian terms, the principle of Incarnation, far from being Revelation (or scandalous), is now a statement of the obvious. Sacraments are immediately comprehensible, as symbols. Materiality, and even particularity, no longer seem problematic.

Sex is paradigmatic, not least in Britain, and not least for Christians (of all shades). What was once the 'spiritual' *bête noire*, is now (characteristically) considered from both the 'technical' and 'spiritual' angles. That they are linked is, however, assumed (even when it is felt necessary specifically to deny the importance of their relationship). They are two perspectives, on a single activity, not two opposing sides (meaning, two moral levels).

The meaning, reality and significance of the spiritual, may be more readily apprehended by some of those whose development in this sphere is being monitored, than by some of those responsible for their education. The generation gap in this area, is comparable to that in information technology. In this respect, the 1980s educational reforms gave belated substance to the mysterious inclusion of 'spiritual' among the aims of the 1944 Act, and carried into every school the sort of 'new age' objectives that had developed in primary education in the 1960s. In the Elizabethan Settlement of 1559, Cranmer had similarly communicated the Reformation to every parish, by attaching the Book of Common Prayer to an Act of Parliament. In each case, the 'babes' and the 'simple' have insights which the 'scribes' and 'pharisees' may have difficulty in grasping.

This new (or revived) understanding of the spiritual arises out of a change in context. The spiritual is now seen as embracing, from a moral and developmental standpoint, the whole of subjectivity. But consciousness itself (in the form of 'feeling', 'intuition', 'emotion' 'psychology', 'symbol') has been elevated from epiphenomenal to foundational status: the Self matters, and therefore I, and the world, exist. Exactly balancing this process of conscientisation (as Marx balanced Freud), is a complementary emphasis upon contextualisation.

The difference between this new form of holistic spirituality, and that to be found in small-scale societies, is that consciousness and context (or morality and technology), although conjoined again, are now seen as distinct. We continue to interact with our environment, but it is our experience of *not* being simply a part of it, that has compelled us to recognise that we are also in fact a part of it. The ultimate moral ontology may be personal development (known to the law as 'human rights'); but it now results in a fundamental division of reality, based on the attribution of sensitivity.

Spiritual education, then, whether in school, church or home, will look to the development of the 'sense of the sacred' in the earliest years, and in all family-type contexts; *and* at the development of the 'encounter with the holy', in the years following puberty, and in all role-playing situations; *and* at the development of the 'commitment to the human' in adulthood, and in all positions of anonymity. As there are different ways of being personal, in the different contexts, so there are different ways to be spiritual - only one of which leads to religion in the 'organised' sense.

The concept of implicit religion, spanning the spectrum of the spiritual and the religious, simultaneously facilitates comparison and contrast.

10   THE FUTURE AND IMPLICIT RELIGION

Studying implicit religion involves constantly asking oneself, or the one(s) being studied, such questions as: What makes them tick? What's his goal in life? And, What is his world-view? What brings him to life? What words are most meaning-full for him - and which are least so? How does she see herself, and what is her ideal for herself? However incomprehensible their behaviour - what did they *think* they were doing it for? What made it right, in their own eyes?

In other words, it is concerned with understanding people, from the point of view of their intentionality, at any and every level of consciousness. I can only confess (the word is carefully chosen) that for me, as for many, that seems to serve as an end-term: it hardly needs, or allows, further justification. However, reasons can be given for the faith that is thus confessed. The reasons are not so much for holding the faith in the first place, as for judging it reason-able, when reflecting upon it. (They could be said to explain how an implicit faith is related to an explicit practice!)

First, some of the reasons for, or advantages of, understanding people better can be listed. For instance, we live in a shrinking world, that hands individuals and groups instruments of unprecedented power for good and/or ill. So such understanding has become a practical necessity. What we do with our understanding is, of course, yet another question. We might use it to further international cooperation - or to try and sell our particular philosophy or product.

However, the increase of mutual understanding appears to be an absolute good. We can take others' understandings 'on board', not in order that they can simply serve our ends, but so that we ourselves may grow as a result. Although John Wesley meant something rather different, we might use his words as our ideal: The world is my parish. Or, turning from space to time, we might take (and expand) Alexander Pope's saying, There is no excuse for a man to be less than three thousand years old. Such growth in our catholicity and humanity can be a springboard for (as well as a consequence of) meditation and contemplation, prayer and worship, intercession and thanksgiving, contrition and adoration.

Secondly, without the contribution that this approach can make, the study of humanity may sometimes seem to be in danger of de-humanising its very subject-matter, by omitting this element of intentionality. If we study the causes of the French Revolution, for instance, we can discover so many economic, psychological, and other reasons for what happened, that we run the risk of forgetting that every participant in that chain of events also had to decide, from time to time, what to say or do, and could have chosen to say or do something different, or even do nothing at all. The implicit religion approach acknowledges that people have Causes (about which they can be very determined), as well as causes (by which they are determined).

Thirdly, in religion we have a possible model to assist our consideration of this nuanced and sensitive area, in which freedom appears to play a part. Nor should we restrict our attention to the western study of religion during these last two or three centuries. The founders and propagators, the guides and practitioners of the religions, over the last two or three millennia, have also been concerned with what people live (and die) for, what brings people to life (and death). We can do better than waiting until people die, before asking what they stand for. By considering them as 'a whole', but from this standpoint, we can avoid treating them as cases, and enjoy the reciprocity of mutual dialogue with them.

Fourthly, the study or consideration of religion itself, demands this extension of concerns (insofar as this broadening does not already happen). For by definition, at least in the opinion of the man-in-the-street (or 'the person-on-the-pavement'), religion must both reflect, and influence, life beyond itself, in order to be, not merely truly religious, but in order to be religious at all. Thus faith, in order to be faith, it is felt, must issue in works. A sacrament cannot be a sacrament unless it is an inter-face between ordinary life and a cosmos that has a sacredness, if only because of its antiquity (or futurity), or size. The sacred may be special and set-apart, but it can only be either of those, in relation to that which is not so special, and from which it is set apart.

but works cannot buy us into heaven!

Fifthly, as modern society evolves into postmodern culture, religiosity in its 'historical' forms becomes an increasingly restricted tool for understanding human behaviour. To understand human behaviour generally, it is necessary to follow where religiosity is leading: to 'spirituality'. Even specifically and explicitly (traditional, organised) religion can only be understood in this way. Peace of mind, etc. is the goal; 'peace with God', if it figures at all, is for our sake, not His.

Lastly, it may be suggested that balance demands this approach. Most religionists will agree that secular approaches, such as the political and sociological, can contribute to our understanding of even such central elements in their tradition as the Council of Nicea or the teachings of the New Testament. So it is hard to find logical justification for the current tradition that secular life should forever be protected from the converse question. Is there something, in some way (possibly some new way(s)), 'religious' about it or in it? To preclude the propriety of the question might itself smack of a taboo, and thus suggest the presence of a sacred - and indicate the relevance of the hypothesis.

APPENDICES

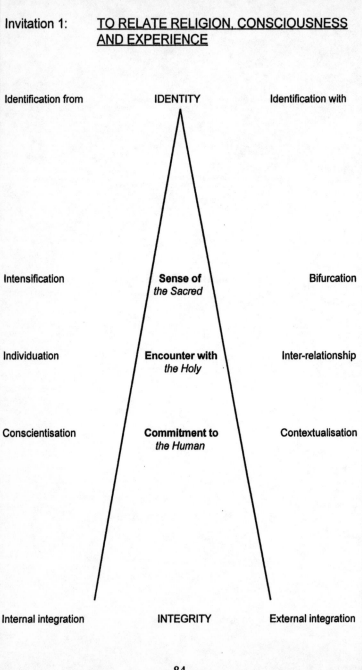

Invitation 1:   <u>TO RELATE RELIGION, CONSCIOUSNESS AND EXPERIENCE</u>

Identification from	IDENTITY	Identification with
Intensification	**Sense of** *the Sacred*	Bifurcation
Individuation	**Encounter with** *the Holy*	Inter-relationship
Conscientisation	**Commitment to** *the Human*	Contextualisation
Internal integration	INTEGRITY	External integration

Invitation 2   <u>TO ANALYSE THE INTERVIEW DATA</u>

A   Motivation

1   What do you enjoy most in life?

  x: Meeting people, reading, watching a good play on television, operas - mainly light ones, especially Gilbert and Sullivan - and helping people!

  y: There's no one pursuit: it's always things of the moment, like drinking and walking, and it depends on my mood. I like a drink with one or two friends, or walking, especially alone.

  z: The children; and being married; and my husband.

2   What makes life worth living?

  x: For me, being married, now, and before that, waiting for it.

  y: To me, now, helping others, because I've realised that I'm not in good health, and many a day I'm not worth a half-penny, but I've got eyes and my daughter Peggy hasn't now - I've got joy in giving.

  z: Understanding that one has a role to play, and so doing the job or performing the role well. I don't feel life is purposeless. In individual situations the individual has responsibilities, and one's job is the recognition of those responsibilities - or doing God's will, in other language.

3   If you had three wishes, and one of them had to be used on yourself but it didn't matter how you used the others, what would you wish?

  x: I'd like good health for myself for the rest of my days. And never to be far from my family. And to have the family come to me for help always.

y: I'd like to do away with all kinds of financial troubles, for myself. And it's worthwhile doing away with wars,

like Vietnam, though this is similar, really, because most wars are over money problems, in some way. And to do away with starvation.

z: I'm so reasonably happy with my circumstances, I don't think of any outstanding wish. I keep saying to myself, I have so much to be thankful for.

4 If you won a lot of money on the Pools (or the Premium Bonds, or whatever), what would you do with it?
(If guidance was asked as to how much, or it was apparent that the respondent was thinking merely in terms of a few hundred pounds, it was mentioned that an enormous sum was in mind, and an advertisement on the side of a bus, saying someone had recently [in 1969] won over £300,000, was quoted.)
x: I'd put a small proportion to one side for the children, including their education. I'd invest a proportion for various purposes, including buying one's own house, and so on. If there was any more, I'd want to give it to people, like Oxfam and Cancer Research, but I'd want it to be more personal - it's a selfish pleasure, but I'd want to give it to situations with which I was familiar.

y: I'd spend a very small proportion of it. I'd give ten per cent immediately to good causes - I've always thought about that. The rest I'd put away.

z: I'd look for some property of my own, and have a really good holiday, and see my parents and my husband's mother were all right.

5 What's the most important thing in life?
x: My wife, of course. Seeing her happy, and the family happy, and retaining our health, and being able to partake in all my activities.

y: Having a circle of friends with whom I can be absolutely at ease and frank.

z: For me, it's family life; for the world, it's love.

6   Is there anything you feel really serious about?

x: Yes, human relationships. The problem is communication, especially between the generations, but also between dons and students, boys and teachers, and in international relations. It's at the root of all manner of problems facing mankind at the moment. It gets me very angry. It's so difficult for the individual to really achieve anything - someone who's really got ideas, but finds it hard to put them across - the individual is submerged. I saw it in America. Students have to resort to demonstrations in order to make the authorities even begin to listen to them.

y: Every situation in which I find people who do not treat other people as individual persons, but only as a category, of things.

z: Yes, I feel seriously about discrimination, over race, for instance. I always find I tend to be on the blacks' side every time there's a fuss over it.

    I suppose you'd say I feel seriously about people's attitudes - I don't just mean their opinions, they're entitled to those, but their attitudes. Like people saying they 'don't like coloureds', without being able to say why, or that 'it's a good thing the Americans are in Vietnam', but they can't give you any reason, when you ask them for one.

7   Does anything ever 'get' you, or move you, or 'send' you whether

(a) angry, annoyed, indignant, fed up, or

(b) pleased, happy, excited, interested?

a:x   People being 'snobby'; and people being 'silly', like girls on buses giggling, though you know they'll grow out of that, or middle-aged women gossiping and cackling - their laughter, ugh! - when they should know better; and people talking loudly.   People being ill-mannered - barging you in the street, or drivers not

waiting for you at pedestrian crossings, and so on.

a:y   Well I'm fed up with my brothers and sisters at the moment.   It's partly my fault, but it's partly theirs, no doubt.   And I don't like being told in front of other people about something you've [sic] done wrong, when I'm out at work.   And I get annoyed with people who are two-faced, rather than straight out.

a:z   Yes, pettiness - often it's my own.   And the 'establishment' - for instance, the examination system in education, and red tape, because it often seems not to regard people - it's meant to be more effective but it isn't always.

b:x   Music certainly gets me.   It's usually only a small snatch out of a piece, such as trumpets, or an orchestra accompanying hymns.   It send shivers down my spine, as if I'm resonant to certain sounds - such as the plaintive clarinet in Acker Bilk's 'Summer Set'.   In art, there's the odd picture, sculpture or film, when you see something deeper than the paint or the music.   I get very turned on, now, to things like drama and films.
Also in everyday life, when suddenly something clicks and a person emerges and says something to you that he means, as an equal person.

b:y   Little things please me very much, like someone coming to see me here at work, or at home, out of their interest.

b:z It's mostly things that happen to me through the children now - watching their development. And friends.

8 What sort of thing do you fear?

x: I must admit I fear death, because I do, but in a very remote way at the moment, though I've a feeling I will fear it more later. I fear dying at an early age, really rather than death itself: having to leave this world with

all its pleasant things.
And of course I fear being a failure, and so on.

y: Getting old, and not being wanted.

z: Yes - I think everyone who works hourly has the threat of redundancy at the back of his mind, always.
And I'm afraid of being senile.
Otherwise, I'll try anything once.

9 What do you dislike most about people - when you find it in them?

x: It's an absence of humility, arrogance, an insensitivity to the opinions of others, self-righteousness, sanctimoniousness, the refusal to recognise that there's a grain of truth in other people's views.

y: I hate people to be unnatural - to be bombastic, or have snobbish ideas - that does strain my tolerance. But I don't worry any more. That's one of the things that has come with age. I've faced so many of the crises that an average person has to face, and have come out all right; but I do sometimes get concerned.

z: I dislike dishonesty of purpose, and of speech - backbiting, for instance. And bad manners, however much the same is true of me. And dirty people.

10 What do you feel most grateful for in life, or most glad about?
- x: For my health and the health of my family. Because I come from a very poor family, and I never imagined I'd live quietly and happily with all the things I needed - I never ask for what I want, but what I need.
And for the opportunity to serve God - I've always considered that a great privilege.
And for my wife.

- y: Meeting and falling in love with my husband, is the great thing, and one's own family background.

- z: The gifts one has been given, without any doubt whatsoever. I feel very sorry for people who've been born without any gifts whatsoever.
And for having a home such as I had, and being born on this island, and other things connected with that. And that I came out of the last War - we should feel eternally grateful for that.

11 Do you ever feel there is anything lacking in your life?
- x: Not really.

- y: Before I was engaged, I would have given you a tirade on that! Now there are only things that are lacking in me - maturity, ideas, strength, and a clear idea of where I'm going.

- z: I wish there was more contact between my parents and myself - I know it's a common complaint of people of my age. I want to be able to sit down and talk with them, but within two minutes it always becomes an argument between my father and myself. Our views are different on everything we discuss - religion, politics, everything - and he can't stand it.

B   World-view

1   What do you feel is the biggest problem in the world?
    x: Managing humanity - I'd go back to Robbie Burns - one
            country against another, and dictatorship. And
            starvation - it could be overcome with the right
            cooperation by people.

    y: Trying to get people of different mentalities to agree, on
            a common level of love and understanding. What a
            lovely world it would be if all nations were ... all
            Christians, if you like. Not that I ever feel hopeless
            about things; nothing's ever as bad as you thought it
            was going to be. That's very true.

    z: The colour-bar and starvation.

2   Do you feel the world is changing for the better or the worse, or
    not at all?
    x: The potentials have increased, but men are not
            necessarily happier. Still, on the whole, there are more
            people who enjoy life more, now, than there were in the
            past.

    y: All in all, for the worse. Man has not reached the
            emotional maturity that's required to use his inventions
            and discoveries in ways that aren't dangerous.

    z: People stay the same.

3   What do you think is the purpose of life?
    (Guidance was frequently asked as to whether this meant 'of
    the whole thing', or 'my purpose', in which case the interviewer
    always reminded the respondent that (s)he was free to take it
    as (s)he wished, and suggested (s)he 'might like to say both'.)
    x: We've been fortunate to have been given a life, and so
            we should try and make it as deep and as wide as
            possible, and to try and make other people happy in the

process.

y: I don't know. I used to see things cosmically, but I don't
        any more. Samuel Beckett had a great influence on me
        about a year and a half ago. I was in a play of his, and
        I'm recovering from it still. I can't accept it absolutely,
        but he says our whole life is just waiting: we're born
        'astride the grave'.

z: The riddle of the universe is still unanswerable, and I
        wouldn't be surprised if it isn't always. As a Christian, I
        would say, To do God's will - whatever that means - it
        isn't always easy to know.

4   When would you like to have been born, if you hadn't been
      born when you were?
      (If the response had not already made it clear, the interviewer
      would   additionally   ask,   'Who   as?   and

      Whereabouts?')
      x: I'd rather not change.

      y: Oh, in Victorian times - the clothes.

      z: Some time later - now, with so many exciting things in
              front of you.
C   Values

1   What would a perfect world be like?
      x: Ha! This ties up with my 'wishes'. My perfect world
              would be in a way, selfish. It would be as it is now, but
              without the tension, and it would be fairly static in
              population, and in the number of cars, and so on.

      y: I haven't any other picture. I don't think it would be
              primitive: modern technology is better.
              Oh gosh! The sun would shine all the time, it would be
              full of happiness, there'd be no cruelty, everyone would

live happily together, there'd be no pain or suffering. Of course, it couldn't possibly be perfect, human nature being what it is. It wouldn't work, because someone would always be dissatisfied. There'd be nothing to work for, and nothing to overcome.

z: I can't visualise it. 'Perfect' is not something you can reach, by definition. If it was perfect by our present ideas, then it wouldn't be so then.

2   If you could change any one thing in the world, what would you change?
(If guidance was sought as to how realistic it had to be, the interviewer replied that it could be   anything, this was 'an abracadabra question'.)
x: I don't know.

y: Wars - or poverty and under-development. I'd have a universal communism, with no strings attached.

z: A lot of problems would be solved if everybody was the same colour.

3   Where is the best place to start putting the world right - not necessarily meaning a geographical place, of course?
x: As an individual, or as the world? In theory, the United Nations sets about doing this, at the world level, and it's the best of what we've got at the moment, though it's fairly unsuccessful so far.
As an individual, the best place to start is where you are.

y: In the home. If only we had some means of making sure that parents, when they married, have a standard home with a sense of reason and proportion - though we don't want to turn out sausages.

z: In schools, with your teaching. Start with the children, and give them the right ideas. What's wrong to a large extent with the present generation is that they don't know what they do want. They must learn about consideration for each other, and helping people, especially those worse off than they are. Many of the youngsters are groping blindly for something to do.

4 Who is most likely ever to put the world right?
x: Not the Government. If people worked in harmony, and did the right thing, they could make it much better.

y: To name Christ would be blasphemous - he doesn't need my vote, he can manage on his own. He is very involved, but we don't understand his role.
So, it's the whole collection of me's.

z: God, through the Church. But that's very idealistic. In practical terms, the leader of the Chinese people - not the present one, of course, but whoever is. There was a time when I put most faith in the United Nations, but that doesn't seem to be doing very well at the moment.

5 What do you think a perfect person would be like?
x: I have come across Christians of whom I would say, 'Here's the most perfect person I've ever met up to now.' But perfection covers, or should cover, so many things. It's just what you'd expect of really good Christians: general sweetness, tolerance, loving in the widest sense.

y: It's a self-contradiction - we're not like dogs in Cruft's.

z: Very dull.
He would not be arrogant, he would be able to communicate, and he'd have the usual qualities of kindness, humility and humanity.

6   Do you see any hope of anyone ever being perfect?
(If the response had not already made it clear, the interviewer would additionally ask, 'Why?', or 'Why not?')

x: No, because I always say, when people criticise other people, 'We're only human, there's got to be something the matter with us'.

y: No, because there is no such thing. The top of the scale must be free, and open. But some people are near it.

z: No, on statistical grounds. It would be like going through the chair you're sitting on. There are too many variables.

7   What would you like your children (or 'your grandchildren', or any other child relatives that had already been spoken of, or 'any children/grandchildren that you had') to be like and to be?
(If guidance was asked as to whether this referred to professions, or character, the interviewer replied that it referred to both.)

x: I would not like them to have the tycoon mentality of grasping and pushing. I'd prefer them to be artistic and musical. I would not want them to be materially ambitious.

y: I don't know. I have no particular ambitions for them. They must be themselves.

z: Just to grow up God-fearing - I mean, if they have a sense of honesty, they can't go far wrong.

8   What's the most useful job in the world - including a housewife, for instance, as a 'job'?

x: There are so many, and every one hangs upon another - the dustman has one of the most useful.

95

y: A doctor, or a teacher - in the widest sense of the word, not just a school-teacher. No, being a parent, especially if they're also a good teacher.

z: Something in the medical field. You can live without a politician, but you must have good health.

D   *Routine*
(This section was frequently introduced with the comment that it had proved difficult to convey the meaning initially, but it now seemed satisfactory, and that it was about the absolutely ordinary, everyday things of life.)

1   Sometimes at the end of a day, you might say it has been a really good day (the interviewer checked for comprehension at this point, but it was always satisfactory, after the evolution of the stimulus in this form): what are the practical things that turn an ordinary day into a really good day?

x: That I've achieved all the tasks that I set off to do in the morning, without difficulty and without trouble.

y: It depends on the various parts of my job being lively, and when things get across to people, and on one's relationships with people, and lack of tension in one's personal relationships on the day itself. That seems to be capricious - you can't plan it, but it depends a lot on your tiredness.

z: You always end the day happier if you've done a job you've been putting off.

2   What do you mean by a 'really good day' - can you find another word to describe it? I was being deliberately vague, in my usual way: can you find something more precise than just 'good'?

x: 'Satisfying' - because, one's achieved something and used the time well, as well as had good relationships.

y: I can't say 'satisfying' yet, because the moment of satisfaction is still two and a half years away, as I'd doing a PhD.

z: 'Occupied' - a day in which I've been engaged in living.

3 Is there any part of the ordinary routine of living which you would really miss if it was abolished - apart from what you need just in order to keep alive?
x: No, I don't think there is anything really.
I'd miss music a great deal, and books, and human company.

y: The chores - it would be terrible to sit idle and not have anything to do.

z: Well, living in such lovely country here, I'd miss not being able to go for a walk every day, or not being able to cut flowers from the garden. And I'd miss sitting in the evening and watching television - when it's good.

4 What is the most important thing you do each year?
x: Going away - abroad - for a holiday. I enjoy it too, but it's my husband's chief thing of the year.
And I like to visit my more far-away relations, and see old friends, which I can usually do each year.

y: I'm not old enough to answer that one yet - the year doesn't have any pattern. Except that for the last five

years, we've had a baby every other year.

z: Exams have been so far in my life, because I've had them every year for ages now. And Christmas. And my birthday, but that's mainly for nostalgic reasons.

5   What is the most important thing you do each week?
x: I like to go to Church. Once a week's enough, just to keep with it, 'in touch'.

y: I wish there was something, but there isn't, because I'm too pragmatic. I take life very much as it comes, and I tend not to look forward to things.

z: To get by and do my bits of jobs.

6   What is the most important thing you do each day?
x: Trying to get out a decent day's work, so everyone is satisfied. Next, it's finishing work, because that's the start of leisure time - that's what I work for.
         I also keep having purges when it's getting up on time, but they don't last long.

y: I can't single out any one thing that's more important than the others I can think of.

z: Praying over things. I used to do it regularly every morning before I had any children. Now I do it at odd times during the day, while I'm washing up and so on.

7   Have you had any embarrassing experiences (as Wilfred Pickles used to say)?
x: I'm sure I must have done, but I don't remember any of them now.

y: Singularly few that I can think of, that were intensely embarrassing.

z: Frequently, such as wetting your pants when you're a child, or forgetting to do certain things, or saying something about a third party who turns out to be

behind your shoulder.

8 Who do you admire most? As I said before we began, it might be one person, or several people, or a 'class' of persons, someone who's dead or alive or purely imaginary, or no one at all.

x: I admire George Bernard Shaw: he wrote such characters, like St Joan. And Barbara Castle, because she has the will-power to get on, and she must know she's unpopular.
And Prince Philip, because he says what he thinks.

y: My father, because he's clever, but never scores off anybody. In many ways he's unappreciated - he's a parson - but he always appears contented. He never appears upset, he appears to have no pride.

z: Churchill. He epitomises what a human being should be like. He had tremendous personality, humour, many talents, ability as a leader which is so bound up with personality, and at the same time lots of human frailties, so he was completely and utterly human. We can read about him and chuckle.
In contrast, I also had great admiration for Eisenhower. But he became rather moralising later - he was slightly too perfect, but he was a close second, because he was totally lacking in any sort of arrogance.

E Beliefs
1 Are there any things that you would say
(a) you definitely do not believe in, or
(b) you definitely do believe in?

a:x I can't think of anything, except for superficial ones, like ghosts.

a:y I don't like the whole idea of 'not believing in' things. I tend to say, 'I just don't know'. It's just too final - ghosts, and ESP, for instance.

a:z   I don't believe in heaven and hell, as places, in God as a Father sitting up there, in ghosts, but I'm not sure about the supernatural, such as telepathy and ESP, or in the value of violence, as fascism does.

b:x   I believe in God, of course, but I don't understand him. In other words, in a sense I would describe myself as a Christian agnostic, as it's now possible to do so.

b:y   I believe in Christianity; and a sense of humour; and honesty.

b:z   I do believe in the ultimate goodness of men. Basically, given the right circumstances, and atmosphere, a person is good.

2   Are there any proverbs or saying that you think
(a) are true, or
(b) are not true?

x: Half of them contradict the other half. I believe in most of them, that are not contradicted by the other half - 'a stitch in time', for instance. There are a lot of wise sayings.

y: I think a lot of them are true. There are so many. For instance, 'a stitch in time', and 'never put off until tomorrow what you can do today'. They're built on common sense. Often one will flash through my mind - like, 'Empty cans make the most noise'.

z: I don't remember any. Being a scientist, I tend to take a rational view, and feel there is some truth in any view.

3   Is there anything which other people seem to believe in and you wish that they didn't?

x: No, let them believe in what they like - who am I to run their beliefs? You can still put your point of view, though. I often do, about ghosts for instance - I watch for them, for the local paper.

y: I wish people didn't believe in [Enoch] Powellism. And in materialism, though I'm as guilty as anybody else. I mean the belief that the car or TV or mortgage are the vital necessities of life. It's all due to insecurity really, and I'm as guilty of that as anyone, but it's the business of keeping up with the Joneses, of caring too much about what other people think, for wrong reasons, that gets me - reasons of prestige, snobbery, position, how it affects them.

I wish people didn't form set prejudices, that they had a tolerant attitude of being prepared to change their views if they're not right. What we need is the 'constant reappraisal' that the Kennedy's talked about.

z: I wish people thought more about the arts, and education - that they were more aware of them.

4 If you were prepared to die for anything, what would it be?
(If the response had not already made it clear, the interviewer would additionally ask, Do you think you would do so?)

x: I think I'm a prize coward, really. I can only see myself dying to rescue my little boy, or my wife, or parents. I'd like to think I would, in other situations too, but one must be realistic about these things. I've never been in the army, but I've thought about that: I can only say, I suppose the best comes out in people, when the crunch comes.

y: I don't want to die for 'any thing', just in general, like that. I'm afraid I'd make a poor Christian martyr, but I wouldn't want to say I wouldn't die for that. I could do something constructive, that may result in my death, but that wouldn't be dying for it.

z: I haven't thought about this particularly, but I think

probably the most likely way would be for a friend, to rescue him, rather than 'for my country' - probably because I would feel my sacrifice was more significant.

5   Supposing you had a minute, just time to say a sentence or two, in which to pass on your philosophy of life to a fifteen year old, what would you say? I say a fifteen year old, because they're old enough to understand what you are saying, without having had your experience of life.
(In the group interviews of teenagers, this was amended to, 'someone a year or two younger than yourself'.)

x: The important thing is the greatest happiness of the greatest number. And Christianity. And being kind to others. And you can't be happy yourself if you don't make other people happy.

y: I would suggest he should be considerate, and have an open mind about things in general, and 'if older people suggest things, don't brush it aside but analyse it and pick out the meat of the advice'.

z: Never be afraid of the truth, about anything and everything, and fear God. It's so easy to scramble out of things with a little lie, but you should own up.

6   What is the most important thing in the world?
(If questioned, the interviewer pointed out that this was not quite the same as A5.)

x: Love and understanding.

y: As a person, I would say good health. For the world, or people as a whole, they ought to have a faith or a belief in something really. Each group would have to develop its own.
(What is your faith or belief, in fact now that you are no longer happy with Roman Catholicism?)
My way of life at the moment is that I want to try and live

at peace with people, and be considerate. I have no very strong feelings about anything in particular - 'live and let live'.

z: To the world at this moment, the most important thing is that every single body of people has to be better than everybody else - the Americans and Russians, for instance.

7   What is the most powerful thing in the world?
    x: Love, and/or hate.

    y: The two Powers, the USA and USSR - their military potential - at the level of 'might is right'. I would like to think it is truth, honesty and loyalty, but they're not, at the moment.

    z: Money, or is it? Is it people trying to do good?
         It's one of them. Of course, money can be used by people to do good - I hadn't thought of it in quite that way before.

8   What is the best thing in the world?
    x: Love.

    y: I can't say, except at the trivial level.

    z: The things that move me most deeply and make me most happy are all related to human loyalty. There are other specific answers, like a Mozart symphony. But I'm prepared to forego music, in order that there may be human kindness, on the same principle as the Atlantic convoys - that all must move at the speed of the slowest.

9   What puzzles you most about life? What sort of things makes you say to yourself, 'I wonder why ...' or 'I can't understand ...'?
    x: I can't understand how people can be unkind and cruel

to children and animals. I know I just couldn't bring myself to do it. I can't understand their being made like that, that they can be so rotten.

y: The biggest puzzle to me, and it must be to anyone who thinks, is, Why we're here at all. I often think, there's no reason why there shouldn't be a universe with inhabitants with a much higher mentality.

z: What a difficult time some people have, and what an easy time others have, though you never can tell,

really.

F Meanings
1 Is there anything that you might be prepared to use the word 'sacred' of?
x: Each person's own beliefs.

y: To me, Jesus is sacred. Our Lord is sacred - he's the most sacred thing in my life.

z: People talk about sacred places, but I wouldn't use it at all.

2 What do you mean or understand by 'sacred'?
x: Something which is personal, which should be cherished, and which you alone have got. This is where I disagree with western religion's organised sacredness together at a set time on Sunday mornings. The Tibetan monk, and the whole Tibetan nation, were so fantastically devout - they even frowned on civilisation, and the wheel, until 1949.

y: It's a belief in something that is almost untouchable, or something that has got to be revered in some way.

z: Those aspects of life which directly, or indirectly, relate to God.

3 What would you mean or understand by 'holy'?

x: The 'sacred' isn't religious, but 'holy' does mean 'religious' to me. I could apply it to everybody's religious symbols. But it's not a word I've clarified yet - it just carries the overtone of incense.

y: It's very close to 'sacred', but again I would understand it in other people's terms. I am impressed by people who are able to see something as holy, such as people who draw strength from a grave. I approve - though my approval is irrelevant, of course - of a personally felt holiness.

z: 'God-fearing' - you can't be a 'holy' man, apart from religion; it's an attitude.

4 Have you had any great moments in your life - the sort you'll never forget?

x: Yes: entering examinations, and passing them, and getting jobs, and getting married, and being present at the birth of one's children, and coming to decisions about things like the way you live and being a Christian.

y: Yes, the revivalist meeting I attended with a school-friend, when I was about sixteen, for one. I had a conversion experience. I didn't used to go to Church often, but I took it more seriously than many of my friends who went regularly, and I had an experience of an abyss at my feet, as if the ground was dropping away. But I couldn't help asking myself whether I was acting it all. I took it extremely seriously, but I gave it up about four weeks later, because I was not in real contact with a church, and I was under a constant strain of being over-conscientious throughout the day. But the effects have continued. For instance, I felt more guilty afterwards about not going to church.

Then there have been some moments in the theatre, even in Gilbert and Sullivan, and with ballet especially - I've sometimes been absolutely enraptured then - and in West Side Story.

Then there have been moments in Germany that I'll never forget. Like walking up a Tiepolo staircase in a Baroque residence in Wurzburg and suddenly hearing an orchestra rehearsing Mozart. And walking into the Baroque cathedral in Salzburg - the whole thing broke on you, as you went through the door, and there was an organ recital going on too, just as though it was all for you. And very often simple things, like a magnificent view, especially in the mountains, or being up on the moors, by myself, or when you seem to be alone - that's partly because of 'Wuthering Heights', which I must have read about eight times since I was twelve years old.

z: The day we were married, when everyone greeted me in such a friendly way; and passing my exams, and the day I'd heard I'd got the job going to sea; and my husband's face, when we decided we were expecting.

5 What, if anything, would you say they've shown you of the meaning of life?

x: I associate their happiness with some insight into what makes life meaningful, what it's about. Raymond Williams' novel 'Border Country', talks about people who had an answer to that, in my opinion.

y: No, they haven't shown me anything really. I haven't found anyone with the same views. I've never been able to sort myself out - I haven't really sorted myself out.

z: Yes. I've learnt the basic pattern of life, from people and from things that have happened. So you learn how to plan your own course.

The basic pattern is that you should be a good, honest person, an active member of the community. It's not easy to put simply. Someone else might say 'To feather your own nest as easily as possible' - that's easy to put. But I don't want to say that, and what I do want to say is not so easy to put.

6   Whether or not you would use the word 'God' yourself, what does the word mean to you?

x: I do use the term 'God', but it is difficult to define. I'd say, There is a God, for want of a better word, whether it be the Buddha, Jesus, Thor, or ...There's definitely a being who is called God.

y: I can't imagine living life without Him. That's enough.

z: In terms of this figure sitting up there watching everything ... I think it's unimportant, but I can't get beyond thinking it's still up there.
I agree with Blake's idea. He's feeling for it, but I don't think it's accepted as orthodox by Christians. I

wouldn't use the word myself, but I have used it, to refer to the 'spirit of humanity', which I think is what Blake means by it. It's to do with spiritual communication between people. It connects with the experience of beauty and so on that we've discussed - with a higher plane of things.

7   What would you mean by 'true religion', so that you might describe a person as 'truly religious'?

x: I think what I mean is ... I don't really know. I know what I mean, but I can't put it into words.
An attitude can be very religious, without going to church. You might still have Church in you, even if you've missed one or two weeks.

y: It's certainly not living in church. It's human acts of kindness and sympathy.

z: I could apply it to someone who's mad keen on cricket. So that means, so long as he carried his religion into all his life.

8   Have you ever known anyone like that?

x: Yes, several - spiritual people. I've great admiration for them. I'm impressed with the fact that they don't try and thrust it onto you.

y: One or two people.

z: I don't think so.

9   If a fifteen year old - again! - came to you and asked you to tell him how he could always distinguish right from wrong, good from bad, what would you say?
      (If asked for further guidance, the interviewer said: "He says, when I was a young child, it was easy to tell the difference, because if my parents told me to do something, it was automatically right, and if they said, Don't, then I knew it was wrong; but now I've no longer got them to tell me, and I've moved away from home, into all sorts of situations, and I

      cannot always tell what is right and what is wrong. Can you give me any sort of rule?")

x: Your conscience will immediately tell you. But you can also ask yourself, Is it done by most people or not? If it is exceptional, then be careful; but if people you respect do it, then it's all right.

y: To what extent does it help other people. The good would help many, the bad may help some.

z: If the fifteen year old knew something of Christianity, I'd say, "Is it in accord with the will of Christ?".

10   And finally: Who are you?
(If guidance was asked in this case, in fact none was given, beyond slowly repeating the question, to allow greater time for it to be comprehended.)

x: What do you mean by that?
        I'm just another human being. I get the feeling my own family might miss me. But I've lived too quiet a life for anyone else to miss me.

y: Yahweh's answer: I am that I am.

z: Will my name do?
        I'm the wife of so-and-so, the housewife of so-and-so...
        I'm a person.
        But what nationality, even, am I, at the moment? I don't even know that at the moment.

Invitation 3   TO FURTHER READING AND STUDY

Having enquired of a leading Religious Studies scholar whether it was possible to do a course in 'Secular Religion' (as I called it in 1968), and discovered that it wasn't, when I met F B Welbourn a little later. I simply asked whether he could recommend any reading on the topic - and was told that nothing had yet been written. Since then, the situation, so far as published literature goes, has changed considerably, although there is still room for a particular publishing house to take this field under its wing. There is a fairly constant, and now fast-growing, output of material that is directly relevant (several hundred items, to my certain knowledge).

However, they await the sort of selectivity and systematisation that could be initiated by an anthology and a full-scale bibliography. So, in the meantime, gatherings such as those arranged since 1978 by the Network for the Study of Implicit Religion, and also from 1998 by the Centre for the Study of Implicit Religion and Contemporary Spirituality, must remain among the best ways of tuning into this wavelength, for much of the most relevant material has not yet been published formally. From 1998, however, the journal *Implicit Religion,* will allow others to take part in these discussions.

One work specifically uses this concept: a shortened but still fairly full version of my own doctoral thesis, *Implicit Religion in Contemporary Society* (Kampen, Netherlands: Kok Pharos, 1997).

Similarly conceptualised, and central to serious study, for those who read Italian or Dutch are: Arnaldo Nesti, *Il Religioso Implicito* (Rome: Januar, 1985), and Meerten ter Borg, *Ein Uitgewaairde Enewigheid: het menselijk tekort in de moderne cultuur* (The Hague: Harm Meijer, 1991). Shorter, but equally relevant, (and also in need of translation) is: Albert Piette, *Les Religiosites Seculières* (Paris: Presses Universitaires, 1993).

Three shorter studies, in English, have already been cited: David Hay, *Exploring Inner Space: scientists and religious experience* (Harmondsworth: Penguin, 1982); Robert Bellah, *Civil Religion in America*, originally published in Daedalus: Journal of the American Academy of Arts and Sciences, XCVI, 1, Winter 1966, and since re-published in (for instance) H W Richardson & D R

Cutler (eds), *The Year Book of Religion* (London: Evans Bros,

1969, with commentaries); and Thomas Luckmann, *The Invisible Religion: the problem of identity in modern society* (London: MacMillan, 1967). Despite the sub-titles given by some publishers to Hay's other works, and the brevity of Bellah's essay (originally, a paper at a conference), and the American-German sociological abstraction of Luckmann's essay, these three are pertinent and pregnant, modern classics.

Three older classics that have also been referred to, which must lie behind all study of religion as a genre (or 'religiosity' as a general phenomenon) are: William James, *The Varieties of Religious Experience: a study in human nature,* 1902 (London: Collins, 1960); Emile Durkheim, *The Elementary Forms of the Religious Life,* 1915 (Glencoe: Free Press, 1947); and Rudolph Otto, *The Idea of the Holy,* 1917 (Harmondsworth: Penguin, 1959). A rather neglected classic, of the developmental psychology of religion, is: Edwin Diller Starbuck, *The Psychology of Religion: an empirical study of the growth of religious consciousness* (London: Scott, 1899).

An overview of, and an anthology illustrating, human religiosity, are Frederick J Streng, *Understanding Religious Man* (Belmont: Dickenson, 1969), and Streng's and others', *Ways of Being Religious: readings for a new approach to religion* (Englewood Cliffs, NJ: Prentice Hall, 1973). How the possibility of a new approach could ever be arrived at, is finely illustrated in Jacques Waardenberg (ed), *Classical Approaches to the Study of Religion: aims, methods and theories of research* (The Hague: Mouton, 1973).

Five more recent works, that include empirical observation, are: Peter L Berger, *A Rumour of Angels: modern society and the re-discovery of the supernatural* (Harmondsworth: Penguin, 1971); Fred Blum, *The Ethics of Industrial Man: an empirical study of religious awareness and the experience of society* (London: Routledge and Kegan Paul, 1970); Paul Halmos, *The Faith of the Counsellors* (London: Constable, 1965); Marghanita Laski, *Ecstasy: a study of some secular and religious experiences* (London: Cresset, 1961); and Michael Paffard, *Inglorious Wordsworths: a study of some transcendental experiences in childhood and adolescence* (London: Hodder and Stoughton, 1973).

With these may be mentioned three shorter pieces that are all reproduced in W A Lessa and E Z Vogt, *Comparative Religion: an anthropological approach* (New York: Harper and Row, 1965). They are: Ralph Linton, *Totemism and the AEF*; Horace Miner, *Body Rituals among the Nacirema*; and W E H Stanner, *The Dreaming*.

Certain stages of life continually re-invoke the need for some such concept as implicit religion. One of them was discussed by Violet Madge, *Children in Search of Meaning* (London: SCM, 1965). Others have been mentioned in connection with the psychology of religion, regarding adolescence and transcendence. The approach of death (and near-death experiences), is also now being studied.

People in certain geographical areas have been studied holistically, with attention to their religion, both explicit and implicit, not least of course by anthropologists. Half a dozen lesser-known works can serve as models, not least for their explicit or implicit comparisons.

Three 'area-studies' are: Michael Mayerfield Bell, *Childerley: nature and morality in a country village* [in southern England] (Chicago: University of Chicago Press, 1994); Genchi Kato, *A Study of Shinto: the religion of the Japanese nation, 1926* (London: Curzon, 1971); Raimundo Panikkar, *Time and Sacrifice: the sacrifice of time and the ritual of modernity* (New York: Springer-Verlag, 1978).

Three descriptions of nationalism, which, along with sport, has frequently been cited as an obvious *locus* for implicit religiosity, are: C C J Hayes, *Nationalism: a religion* (New York: MacMillan, 1961); E B Koenker, *Secular Salvations: the rites and symbols of political religions* (Philadelphia: Fortress, 1965); and John E Smith, *Quasi-religions: Humanism, Marxism, Nationalism* (New York: St Martin's, 1994).

Three other discussions of particular topics are: Jeffrey F Meyer, *The Dragons of Tiananmen: Beijing as a sacred city* (Columbia: University of Carolina Press, 1991); Kathryn Allen Rabuzzi, *The Sacred and the Feminine: towards a theology of housework* (New York: Seabury, 1982); and Philip Sherrard, *The Sacred in Life and Art* (Ipswich: Golgonooza Press, 1990).

More general and theoretical introductions, from particular points of view, are found in: Mary Douglas, *Purity and Danger: an analysis of concepts of purity and taboo* (Harmondsworth: Penguin, 1970); Hans Mol, *Identity and the Sacred: a sketch for a*

new social-scientific study of religion (Oxford: Blackwell, 1976); The Journal of Oriental Studies, XXVI, 1, 1987, *Feature: beyond the dichotomy of secularity and religion.*

Lastly, Lynda Sexson, *Ordinarily Sacred* (London: University of Virginia Press, 1992), is a pleasantly 'popular' yet 'neutral' survey of the area. However, most general (and most profound?) of all, for the study of all religion (explicit or implicit), may be Stanley A Cook's article, *Religion*, in the J J Hastings (ed.) *Encyclopaedia of Religion and Ethics* (Edinburgh: T & T Clark, 1918), Vol X:662-693.